D1603949

DAILY
JOY

A DEVOTIONAL FOR
EACH DAY OF THE YEAR

DAILY
JOY

RUSSELL M. NELSON

DESERET
BOOK

SALT LAKE CITY, UTAH

Book design © Deseret Book Company
Cover image: Westend61/Getty Images

© 2020 Russell M. Nelson

DESERET BOOK is a registered trademark of Deseret Book Company.

Visit us at deseretbook.com

Library of Congress Cataloging-in-Publication Data
(CIP data on file)
ISBN 978-1-62972-830-8

Printed in China
RR Donnelley, Dongguan, China

10   9   8   7   6   5   4   3   2   1

JANUARY

Therefore, dearly beloved
brethren, let us cheerfully do
all things that lie in our power;
and then may we stand still,
with the utmost assurance, to
see the salvation of God, and
for his arm to be revealed.

DOCTRINE AND COVENANTS 123:17

HOPE FROM HIM WHO IS ETERNAL

Now the God of hope fill you with all joy and peace in believing, that ye may abound in hope, through the power of the Holy Ghost.

ROMANS 15:13

As we begin a new year, we desire to improve our talents—by the patience of hope and the labor of love. We all have hope. . . . Hope emanates from the Lord, and it transcends the bounds of this mortal sphere. Paul noted that "if in this life only we have hope in Christ, we are of all men most miserable" (1 Corinthians 15:19). Only with an eternal perspective of God's great plan of happiness can we ever find a more excellent hope. . . . Have you heard the old statement that "hope springs eternal"? It can only be true if that hope springs from Him who is eternal.

FREE TO CHOOSE

Behold, here is wisdom, and let every man
choose for himself until I come.

DOCTRINE AND COVENANTS 37:4

Why are you here on planet earth?

One of the most important reasons is to receive a mortal body. Another is to be tested—to experience mortality—to determine what you will do with life's challenging opportunities. Those opportunities require you to make choices, and choices depend on agency. A major reason for your mortal existence, therefore, is to test how you will exercise your agency.

Agency is a divine gift to you. You are free to choose what you will be and what you will do. . . . The proper exercise of moral agency requires faith. Faith in the Lord Jesus Christ is the first principle of the gospel. Because of Him, you have your agency. He must be the very foundation of your faith, and the testing of that faith is a fundamental reason for your freedom to choose.

GOD'S ETERNAL PLAN

Adam did fall by the partaking of the forbidden fruit, according to the word of God; and thus we see, that by his fall, all mankind became a lost and fallen people. . . . Therefore this life became a probationary state; a time to prepare to meet God; a time to prepare for that endless state which has been spoken of by us, which is after the resurrection of the dead.

ALMA 12:22, 24

The *Creation* of the earth and all that dwell therein, the necessary *Fall* that enabled man to be, and the *Atonement* of the Lord are three fundamental components of God's eternal plan. Without that atoning sacrifice, there would be neither immortality nor eternal life.

His message *is* the restored gospel of Jesus Christ; and it is administered by the Church that bears His name. He directs the affairs of His church by the power of the priesthood and by revelation through prophets who proclaim His doctrine to all people of the world.

SPIRITUAL POWER

*And it came to pass that I, Nephi, beheld that the Gentiles
who had gone forth out of captivity did humble themselves
before the Lord; and the power of the Lord was with them.*

1 NEPHI 13:16

The source of our spiritual power is the Lord! The ultimate source of spiritual power is God our Father. The messenger of this power is the Holy Ghost. . . .

Our spiritual power line is strengthened through prayer. As we counsel with God in all our doings, he will direct us for good. Prayer is available whenever we ask for it! But the Lord places the initiative upon us. He expects us to reach for His power, just as we must insert the plug in the outlet for electricity. . . . Personal worthiness and scripture study enable us to do more with this power.

Rewards result from the righteous use of the spiritual power belonging to the priesthood!

SINGLE TO THE GLORY

*The light of the body is the eye: if therefore thine eye
be single, thy whole body shall be full of light.*

MATTHEW 6:22

Imagine, if you will, a pair of powerful binoculars. Two separate optical systems are joined together with a gear to focus two independent images into one three-dimensional view. . . . Let the scene on the left side of your binoculars represent *your perception* of your task. Let the picture on the right side represent the *Lord's* perspective of your task—the portion of His plan He has entrusted to you. Now, connect your system to His. By mental adjustment, fuse your focus. Something wonderful happens. Your vision and His are now the same. You have developed an "eye single to the glory of God" (Doctrine and Covenants 4:5). . . . That special vision will . . . help clarify your wishes when they may be a bit fuzzy and out of focus with God's hopes for your divine destiny.

ACHIEVING THE IMPOSSIBLE

For with God nothing shall be impossible.

LUKE 1:37

I feel impressed to counsel those engaged in personal challenges to do right. In particular, my heart reaches out to those who feel discouraged by the magnitude of their struggle. Many shoulder heavy burdens of righteous responsibility which, on occasion, seem so difficult to bear. I have heard those challenges termed *impossible.* . . .

How is it possible to achieve the "impossible"? Learn and obey the teachings of God. From the holy scriptures, heaven-sent lift will be found for heaven-sent duties.

SOURCE OF THE ATONEMENT

Even as the Son of man came not to be ministered unto,
but to minister, and to give his life a ransom for many.

MATTHEW 20:28

Under the Father's great eternal plan, it is the Savior who suffered. It is the Savior who broke the bands of death. It is the Savior who paid the price for our sins and transgressions and blots them out on condition of our repentance. It is the Savior who delivers us from physical and spiritual death.

There is no amorphous entity called "the Atonement" upon which we may call for succor, healing, forgiveness, or power. Jesus Christ is the source. Sacred terms such as *Atonement* and *Resurrection* describe what the Savior did, according to the Father's plan, so that we may live with hope in this life and gain eternal life in the world to come. The Savior's atoning sacrifice—the central act of all human history—is best understood and appreciated when we expressly and clearly connect it to Him.

POWER OF THE
BOOK OF MORMON

*And for this very purpose are these plates preserved,
which contain these records—that the promises of the
Lord might be fulfilled, which he made to his people.*

DOCTRINE AND COVENANTS 3:19

When I think of the Book of Mormon, I think of the word *power*. The truths of the Book of Mormon have the *power* to heal, comfort, restore, succor, strengthen, console, and cheer our souls.

My dear brothers and sisters, I promise that as you prayerfully study the Book of Mormon *every day,* you will make better decisions—*every day.* I promise that as you ponder what you study, the windows of heaven will open, and you will receive answers to your own questions and direction for your own life. I promise that as you daily immerse yourself in the Book of Mormon, you can be immunized against the evils of the day.

LOVE ANCHORED
IN JESUS CHRIST

And thou shalt love the Lord thy God with all thine heart, and with all thy soul, and with all thy might.

DEUTERONOMY 6:5

Love for family and friends, great as it may be, is much more profound when firmly anchored in the love of Jesus Christ. Parental love for children has more meaning here and hereafter because of Him. All loving relationships are elevated in Him. Love of our Heavenly Father and Jesus Christ provides the illumination, inspiration, and motivation to love others in a loftier way.

GODLINESS VANQUISHES PRIDE

If my people, which are called by my name, shall humble themselves, and pray, and seek my face, and turn from their wicked ways; then will I hear from heaven, and will forgive their sin, and will heal their land.

2 CHRONICLES 7:14

Godliness is not a product of perfection; it comes of concentration and consecration. Godliness characterizes each of you who truly loves the Lord. You are constantly mindful of the Savior's atonement and rejoice in His love. Meanwhile you vanquish personal pride and vain ambition. You consider your accomplishments important only if they help establish His kingdom on earth.

STUDY JESUS CHRIST

Behold, I am he who was prepared from the foundation of the world to redeem my people. Behold, I am Jesus Christ. I am the Father and the Son. In me shall all mankind have life, and that eternally, even they who shall believe on my name; and they shall become my sons and my daughters.

ETHER 3:14

Commence [now] to consecrate a portion of your time each week to studying *everything* Jesus said and did as recorded in the Old Testament, for He is the Jehovah of the Old Testament. Study His laws as recorded in the New Testament, for He is its Christ. Study His doctrine as recorded in the Book of Mormon, for there is no book of scripture in which His mission and His ministry are more clearly revealed. And study His words as recorded in the Doctrine and Covenants, for He continues to teach His people in this dispensation.

ANSWERS TO PRAYERS

And it shall come to pass, that whosoever shall call on the name of the Lord shall be saved.

ACTS 2:21

I recognize that, on occasion, some of our most fervent prayers may seem to go unanswered. We wonder, "Why?" I know that feeling! I know the fears and tears of such moments. But I also know that our prayers are never ignored. Our faith is never unappreciated. I know that an all-wise Heavenly Father's perspective is much broader than is ours. While we know of our mortal problems and pain, He knows of our immortal progress and potential. If we pray to know his will and submit ourselves to it with patience and courage, heavenly healing can take place in His own way and time.

OUR SIGNIFICANT ROLE

*Our father hath not spoken of our seed alone, but also
of all the house of Israel, pointing to the covenant which
should be fulfilled in the latter days; which covenant
the Lord made to our father Abraham, saying: In thy
seed shall all the kindreds of the earth be blessed*

1 NEPHI 15:18

When we know who we are and what God expects of us, we are filled with hope and made aware of our significant role in His great plan of happiness. The day in which we now live was foreseen even *before* Jesus Christ was born. . . .

These are [the] latter days. We are the ones foredetermined and foreordained to fulfill that promise. We are the seed of Abraham, Isaac, and Jacob. We are, in fact, the hope of Israel. We are God's treasure, reserved for our particular place and time.

OUR TURN
ON EARTH

For behold, this life is the time for men to prepare
to meet God; yea, behold the day of this life is
the day for men to perform their labors.

ALMA 34:32

Our turn on earth is so new—so exciting—so full of adventure. Sometimes it is difficult for us to realize that the world is pretty old and that the challenges we face are old too. We are newcomers on a very old stage. The plot of the drama is already well written. We enter, prepare for performance, and then brace ourselves for the final curtain call. Our turn on the stage of life's theater is now—a special and an exciting opportunity.

PREDICTABLE
CONSEQUENCES

Now, the decrees of God are unalterable; therefore, the way is
prepared that whosoever will may walk therein and be saved.

ALMA 41:8

Entrapments designed by Satan can *only* bring you misery and spiritual captivity and death. This is true *every* time. The sad consequences of yielding to Lucifer's lures are predictable, dependable, repeatable, and regrettable.

Conversely I promise that as you keep God's commandments, as you live by His laws, you will become increasingly free. This freedom will unveil to you your divine nature and allow you to prosper personally. You will be free from the bondage of sin. You will be free to be you, an effective, righteous leader. You will be prepared to lead by precept and by example, wherever you are needed. Happily, the blessings of keeping God's commandments are also predictable, dependable, and repeatable.

EDUCATION IS SACRED

Take fast hold of instruction; let her not go:
keep her; for she is thy life.

PROVERBS 4:13

Your mind is precious! It is sacred. Therefore, the education of one's mind is also sacred. Indeed, education is a religious responsibility. . . .

Our Creator expects His children everywhere to gain an education as a personal endeavor. . . . When you leave this frail existence, your material possessions will remain here, but the Lord has declared that the knowledge you acquire here will rise with you in the resurrection. In light of this celestial perspective, if you . . . cut short your education, you would not only disregard a divine decree but also abbreviate your own eternal potential.

THE LORD'S DAY

The sabbath was made for man, and not man for the sabbath:
therefore the Son of man is Lord also of the sabbath.

MARK 2:27–28

We proclaim the Sabbath as the Lord's day. We joyfully praise it as a day of delight, at home and at church. . . . We proclaim it as a day when we can truly increase our faith in the Lord and strengthen our families. As our Saints learn to keep the Sabbath day holy, and do it with delight, their capacity to obey *all* the other commandments will be greatly increased.

BLESSINGS OF THE PRIESTHOOD

The power and authority of the higher,
or Melchizedek Priesthood, is to hold the keys of
all the spiritual blessings of the church.

DOCTRINE AND COVENANTS 107:18

Available to each of you brethren and sisters are blessings obtained through the power of the holy Melchizedek Priesthood. These blessings can change the circumstances of your lives, in matters such as health, companionship of the Holy Ghost, personal relationships, and opportunities for the future. The power and authority of this priesthood holds the keys to all spiritual blessings of the Church. And most remarkably, the Lord has declared that He will sustain those blessings, according to His will.

The greatest of all the blessings of the priesthood are bestowed in holy temples of the Lord. Fidelity to covenants made there will qualify you and your family for the blessings of eternal life.

TOLERANCE IS
THE KEY

I . . . beseech you that ye walk worthy of the vocation
wherewith ye are called, with all lowliness and meekness,
with longsuffering, forbearing one another in love.

EPHESIANS 4:1–2

Intolerance seeds contention; tolerance supersedes contention. Tolerance is the key that opens the door to mutual understanding and love. . . . Our commitment to the Savior causes us to scorn sin yet heed His commandment to love our neighbors. Together we live on this earth, which is to be tended, subdued, and shared with gratitude. Each of us can help to make life in this world a more pleasant experience. . . .

Together we may stand intolerant of transgression but tolerant of neighbors with differences they hold sacred. Our beloved brothers and sisters throughout the world are *all* children of God. He is our Father. His Son, Jesus, is the Christ. His Church has been restored to the earth in these latter days to bless all of God's children.

24/7 DISCIPLESHIP

Ye are my disciples;
and ye are a light unto this people.

3 NEPHI 15:12

As disciples, each of us will be put to the test. At any hour of any day, we have the privilege of choosing between right and wrong. This is an age-old battle that started in a premortal realm. And that battle is becoming more intense every day. Your individual strength of character is needed now more than ever before.

The day is gone when you can be a quiet and comfortable Christian. Your religion is not just about showing up for church on Sunday. It is about showing up as a true disciple from Sunday morning through Saturday night—24/7! There is no such thing as a part-time disciple of the Lord Jesus Christ.

RECOGNIZE THE CREATOR

So God created man in his own image, in the image of
God created he him; male and female created he them.

GENESIS 1:27

Under the direction of the Father, Jesus bore the responsibility of Creator. . . . This hallowed Creator provided that each of us may have a physical body, uniquely individual yet in many respects comparable to every other human body. Just as a well-educated musician can recognize the composer of a symphony by its style and structure, so a well-educated surgeon can recognize the Creator of human beings by the similarity of style and structure of our anatomy. Individual variations notwithstanding, this similarity provides additional evidence and deep spiritual confirmation of our divine creation by our same Creator. It enhances the understanding of our relationship to Him.

INCREASED WILLPOWER

Watch and pray, that ye enter not into temptation:
the spirit indeed is willing, but the flesh is weak.

MATTHEW 26:41

Both spirit and body have appetites. One of life's great challenges is to develop a dominance of spiritual appetites over those that are physical. Your willpower becomes strong when joined with the will of the Lord.

Addiction to any substance enslaves not only the physical body but the spirit as well. Therefore, repentance is best achieved while one still has a body to help attain spiritual supremacy.

GO WITH FAITH

I will go and do the things which the Lord hath commanded, for I know that the Lord giveth no commandments unto the children of men, save he shall prepare a way for them that they may accomplish the thing which he commandeth them.

1 NEPHI 3:7

Prior to our birth, . . . I suspect we were terrified, at first, when told we would forget Father, friends, and facts we formerly knew so well. I can believe we were calmed when informed our Father in Heaven would provide prophets and scriptures to guide us and would provide a means whereby we could communicate with Him through prayer and the spirit of revelation. But still we may have been a bit insecure when we learned that faith—faith to believe the intangible—was the key to success in our journey. . . .

Each one of us will have to go to unique testing grounds of faith. . . . For the monument of your life to rise from its pedestal of preparation to your appointed site of destiny, you must go where the Lord wants you to go. Wherever it is, go. Go with the same faith that allowed you to leave your heavenly home in the first place.

A LONG-RANGE VIEW

But learn that he who doeth the works of
righteousness shall receive his reward, even peace in
this world, and eternal life in the world to come.

DOCTRINE AND COVENANTS 59:23

Your life will be a blessed and a balanced experience if you first honor your identity and priority. Keep a good long-range view, knowing that the days of retirement from your work will come. There will also be an end to your mortal life. For hale and hardy young adults, those realities seem pretty remote—about the last things you worry about. But the day of your demise is coming, and eventually you will stand before the Lord in judgment. Contemplation of life after retirement and life after death can help you deal with contemporary challenges.

FULFILLMENT AND JOY

Herein is my Father glorified, that ye bear much fruit; so shall ye be my disciples.

JOHN 15:8

Live as a disciple of the Lord Jesus Christ. Acquire His qualities of civility and concern for others. Learn to reach out, to lift and encourage people. As you cultivate qualities of kindness, courtesy, and respect for others, your life's work will be more fulfilling than if you were to pursue goals strictly with an eye single to your own glory.

Enduring joy comes neither from amassing material wealth nor in doing reportable deeds. True joy comes from becoming all that you may become. Your potential for personal greatness will be enhanced as you come unto Christ and become one with Him.

THE TRUE TEACHER

But ye shall receive power, after that
the Holy Ghost is come upon you.

ACTS 1:8

The Holy Ghost is always the true teacher. We capture that power when we relate our own experiences and bear our own heart-felt testimonies. The Holy Ghost will facilitate the commitment needed for one to love God, to come unto Christ and become one of His covenant keepers. Spiritual communication and true conversion are accomplished through the power of the Holy Ghost.

TREE OF LIFE

He that hath an ear, let him hear what the Spirit saith unto
the churches; To him that overcometh will I give to eat of the
tree of life, which is in the midst of the paradise of God.

REVELATION 2:7

Olive trees are special in the Holy Land. The olive branch is universally regarded as a symbol of peace. This tree provides food, light, heat, lumber, ointments, and medicine. It is now, as it was then, crucial to life in Israel. It is not a deciduous tree, but everbearing—always green. Even if the tree is chopped down, life will spring from its roots, suggesting everlasting life. Jewish tradition often refers to the olive tree as the tree of life. To me it seems to prefigure the Resurrection.

BENEFICIARIES
OF CREATION

For it is expedient that I, the Lord, should make every
man accountable, as a steward over earthly blessings,
which I have made and prepared for my creatures. I, the
Lord, stretched out the heavens, and built the earth, my
very handiwork; and all things therein are mine.

DOCTRINE AND COVENANTS 104:13–14

As beneficiaries of the divine Creation, what shall we do? We should care for the earth, be wise stewards over it, and preserve it for future generations. And we are to love and care for one another.

We are to be creators in our own right—builders of an individual faith in God, faith in the Lord Jesus Christ, and faith in His Church. We are to build families and be sealed in holy temples. We are to build the Church and kingdom of God upon the earth. We are to prepare for our own divine destiny—glory, immortality, and eternal lives. These supernal blessings can all be ours, through our faithfulness.

SPIRITUAL NOURISHMENT

And it shall come to pass that the righteous shall be gathered out from among all nations, and shall come to Zion, singing with songs of everlasting joy.

DOCTRINE AND COVENANTS 45:71

Music has power to provide spiritual nourishment. It has healing power. It has power to facilitate worship; it allows us to contemplate the Atonement and the Restoration of the gospel with its saving principles and exalting ordinances. Music provides power for us to express prayerful thoughts and bear testimony of sacred truths.

Music has power to overcome language barriers. In my experience, some of the most moving congregational singing has been rendered in languages that are foreign to me. Yet it spoke strongly to my soul.

THE BATTLE
FOR TRUTH

*For his merciful kindness is great toward us: and the truth
of the Lord endureth for ever. Praise ye the Lord.*

PSALM 117:2

We live in an exciting time. Some things have never
been better. This is an age of easy access to information—
unprecedented, really. Our ease of communication and
transportation would leave our pioneer forefathers in
breathless envy. . . . And some things have never been
scarier. The nightly news is stoked with reports of grief,
cruelty, and terror. . . .

We live in a time when more and more people deny
God and reject His commandments. The battle for truth
and righteousness becomes the burden of us who love the
Lord and rejoice in the freedom provided by obedience
to His commandments. As His disciples, we proclaim
truth that has withstood the test of time.

OPPOSITION IN ALL THINGS

And no one can assist in this work except he shall be humble and full of love, having faith, hope, and charity, being temperate in all things, whatsoever shall be entrusted to his care.

DOCTRINE AND COVENANTS 12:8

We know that there is an opposition in all things. Not surprisingly, therefore, faith, hope, and charity have their opposing forces. . . . The antithesis of faith is doubt; the opposite of hope is despair. And the counterpart of charity—the pure love of Christ—is disregard or even disdain for Him and His commandments.

Therefore, in our quest for faith, hope, and charity, we must beware of the dangers of doubt, despair, or disdain for the divine.

FEBRUARY

Fulfil ye my joy, that ye be
likeminded, having the same love,
being of one accord, of one mind.

PHILIPPIANS 2:2

CONSTANT JOY

The righteous, the saints of the Holy One of Israel, they who have believed in the Holy One of Israel, they who have endured the crosses of the world, and despised the shame of it, they shall inherit the kingdom of God, which was prepared for them from the foundation of the world, and their joy shall be full forever.

2 NEPHI 9:18

Just as the Savior offers peace that "passeth all understanding" (Philippians 4:7), He also offers an intensity, depth, and breadth of joy that defy human logic or mortal comprehension. For example, it doesn't seem possible to feel joy when your child suffers with an incurable illness or when you lose your job or when your spouse betrays you. Yet that is precisely the joy the Savior offers. His joy is constant, assuring us that our "afflictions shall be but a small moment" and be consecrated to our gain (Doctrine and Covenants 121:7).

CHILDREN OF THE COVENANT

And thy seed shall be as the dust of the earth, and thou shalt spread abroad to the west, and to the east, and to the north, and to the south: and in thee and in thy seed shall all the families of the earth be blessed.

GENESIS 28:14

We are . . . children of the covenant. We have received, as did they of old, the holy priesthood and the everlasting gospel. Abraham, Isaac, and Jacob are our ancestors. We are of Israel. We have the right to receive the gospel, blessings of the priesthood, and eternal life. Nations of the earth will be blessed by our efforts and by the labors of our posterity. The literal seed of Abraham and those who are gathered into his family by adoption receive these promised blessings—predicated upon acceptance of the Lord and obedience to his commandments.

DIVINE LOVE

Let all your things be done with charity.

1 CORINTHIANS 16:14

Jesus asked us to love one another as He has loved us. Is that possible? Can our love for others really approach divine love? Yes it can! The pure love of Christ is granted to all who seek and qualify for it. Such love includes service and requires obedience. . . .

Divine love is perfect, infinite, enduring, and universal. The full flower of divine love and our greatest blessings from that love are conditional—predicated upon our obedience to eternal law. I pray that we may qualify for those blessings and rejoice forever.

PERFECTION THROUGH JESUS CHRIST

Let your heart therefore be perfect with the Lord our God, to walk in his statutes, and to keep his commandments, as at this day.

1 KINGS 8:61

You can attain a certain degree of perfection in some things in this life. And you can become perfect in keeping various commandments. But the Lord was not necessarily asking for your errorless and perfect behavior in all things. He was pleading for more than that. His hopes are for your full potential to be realized: to become as He is! . . . So while you earnestly strive for continuing improvement in your life here, remember that your resurrection, exaltation, completion, and perfection await you in the life to come. That precious promise of perfection could not have been possible without the Lord's Atonement and example.

DEATH IS TEMPORARY

And God shall wipe away all tears from their eyes; and there shall be no more death, neither sorrow, nor crying, neither shall there be any more pain: for the former things are passed away.

REVELATION 21:4

Life does not begin with birth, nor does it end with death. Prior to our birth, we dwelled as spirit children with our Father in Heaven. There we eagerly anticipated the possibility of coming to earth and obtaining a physical body. Knowingly we wanted the risks of mortality, which would allow the exercise of agency and accountability. . . . But we regarded the returning home as the best part of that long-awaited trip, just as we do now. Before embarking on any journey, we like to have some assurance of a round-trip ticket. Returning from earth to life in our heavenly home requires passage through—and not around—the doors of death. . . .

Some facetiously state that nothing is as permanent as death. Not so! The grip of physical death is temporary. It began with the Fall of Adam; it ended with the Atonement of Jesus the Christ.

RESTITUTION FOR SIN

For I will declare mine iniquity;
I will be sorry for my sin.

PSALM 38:18

Why can we not atone for our own wrongs? Often we can. And if we can, we should. Restitution is part of repentance. If you threw a ball through a plate-glass window, you could have the window replaced and make it look good as new again. Stolen money can be returned. But sometimes full restitution simply cannot be made without help. If one has robbed an individual of virtue, or of life itself, personal restitution is not possible. Jesus died to provide that help—to pay the price—so that repentance, peace, and forgiveness could come to a sinner.

COVENANT KEEPER

If ye will obey my voice indeed, and keep my covenant, then ye shall be a peculiar treasure unto me above all people: for all the earth is mine.

EXODUS 19:5

When we realize that we are children of the covenant, we know who we are and what God expects of us. His law is written in our hearts. He is our God and we are His people. Committed children of the covenant remain steadfast, even in the midst of adversity. When that doctrine is deeply implanted in our hearts, even the sting of death is soothed and our spiritual stamina is strengthened.

The greatest compliment that can be earned here in this life is to be known as a covenant keeper. The rewards for a covenant keeper will be realized both here and hereafter.

SPIRIT AND BODY

But there is a spirit in man: and the inspiration
of the Almighty giveth them understanding.

JOB 32:8

You consist of two parts—your physical body, and your spirit which lives within your body. . . . Both are of great importance. Your physical body is a magnificent creation of God. It is his temple as well as yours, and must be treated with reverence. . . .

Remarkable as your body is, its prime purpose is even of greater importance—to serve as tenement for your spirit. . . . Your spirit acquired a body at birth and became a soul to live in mortality through periods of trial and testing. Part of each test is to determine *if* your body can become mastered by the spirit that dwells within it.

DAILY PRACTICE OF FAITH

He that receiveth my law and doeth it, the same is
my disciple; and he that saith he receiveth it and
doeth it not, the same is not my disciple.

DOCTRINE AND COVENANTS 41:5

As we repent and live in accordance with the commandments of God, the Atonement of Jesus Christ becomes a force for permanent change in our lives. We become more pure in heart and true disciples of the Master. Personal prayer, contributions of tithes and offerings, honoring the Sabbath day, and partaking of the sacrament of the Lord's Supper are all regular practices that protect us from the bondage of sin and bring us true freedom and joy.

The daily practice of our faith is not confined solely to religious rites. We reach out to aid the communities in which we live. For example, parent-teacher associations, public schools, and similar worthy civic activities receive our support.

ABRAHAMIC TRIALS

Therefore, they must needs be chastened and tried,
even as Abraham, who was commanded to offer
up his only son. For all those who will not endure
chastening, but deny me, cannot be sanctified.

DOCTRINE AND COVENANTS 101:4–5

God has always asked His covenant children to do difficult things. Because you are covenant-keeping sons and daughters of God, living in the latter part of these latter days, the Lord will ask *you* to do difficult things. You can count on it—Abrahamic tests did not stop with Abraham. . . .

How will you accomplish the impossible? By doing whatever it takes to strengthen your faith in Jesus Christ, by increasing your understanding of the doctrine taught in His restored Church, and by relentlessly seeking truth. When asked to do impossible things, you . . . will be able to step forward with faith and dogged persistence and cheerfully do all that lies in your power to fulfill the purposes of the Lord.

SYMBOLIZING OUR COVENANT

It is expedient that the church meet together often to partake of bread and wine in the remembrance of the Lord Jesus.

DOCTRINE AND COVENANTS 20:75

The importance of an inward commitment to the Lord is symbolized as we partake of the sacrament. Contrast it to other promises made in life, usually symbolized by an outward sign, such as a raised hand or a written signature. The Lord has invited us to symbolize our covenant with Him by a sign that is inward as well as outward. When the sacred emblems of His flesh and blood are administered to us, we are invited to take them into our bodies. As we do, His atoning sacrifice literally becomes a part of our own identity.

One day you will be asked if you took upon yourself the name of Jesus Christ and if you were faithful to that covenant. The newest convert makes the same covenant that each of us has made, to take upon us the Lord's name. We are all allowed—even encouraged—to achieve the fulness of the stature of Christ (see Ephesians 4:13).

CITADELS OF STABILITY

Let your light so shine before men, that they may see your good works, and glorify your Father which is in heaven.

MATTHEW 5:16

You enter a world caught in a steep, slippery slide of diminishing moral values. Against that backdrop, your character and integrity will let you stand out and shine like a lighthouse. If you are true and faithful, you will stand out in stark contrast to the surrounding masses mired in mediocrity. You will be anchored to eternal truth. You, your families, and your homes will become beacons of hope in a darkened world. You will be seen as citadels of stability wherever you live. Your faith and optimism will make you leaders in your communities, in your countries, and in the kingdom of God on earth.

THE CAPACITY TO KNOW

*That by him, and through him, and of him, the worlds
are and were created, and the inhabitants thereof
are begotten sons and daughters unto God.*

DOCTRINE AND COVENANTS 76:24

As mortal beings, we are all—by direct inheritance—
spirit children of our Heavenly Father. There persists in
every human being, from our premortal life, the capacity to know and to respond to the voice of our Father
through the promptings of the Spirit. . . .

In teaching people of many lands, I have learned that
they will respond to the word of their Father regardless
of their nationality, race, or language. The fact is, children know the voice of their Father and they recognize
His truth. That connecting communication comes of the
Spirit.

REAL LOVE

*And walk in love, as Christ also hath loved us,
and hath given himself for us an offering and a
sacrifice to God for a sweetsmelling savour.*

EPHESIANS 5:2

Love does not focus on what someone cannot do. Real love focuses on what someone can do. Love highlights unique qualities that are part of the divine heritage of every son and daughter of God. And beyond that, love flings open the gates of service, which lead to the sweet fields of fulfillment and understanding. There our joy is complete when the time ultimately comes for us to step aside and watch our loved ones at last able to work and willingly serve others as we had first served them.

THE INVITATION

Come unto Christ, and be perfected in him, and deny yourselves
of all ungodliness; and if ye shall deny yourselves of all ungodliness,
and love God with all your might, mind and strength, then is his
grace sufficient for you, that by his grace ye may be perfect in Christ.

MORONI 10:32

We extend an invitation to come unto Christ and to participate in the eternal plan of God. It is an invitation to participate in the ordinances, covenants, and blessings of the holy temple with our families—past, present, and future. . . . That's our objective; that's why we have missionary work. It's that objective of eternal life that we're interested in. It's an invitation to dwell in His holy presence, with the Lord, and with our families forever!

COMBATTING CONTENTION

*And it came to pass that there was no contention
in the land, because of the love of God which
did dwell in the hearts of the people.*

4 NEPHI 1:15

What can we do to combat [the] canker of contention? What steps may each of us take to supplant the spirit of contention with a spirit of personal peace? . . . Personal peace is reached when one, in humble submissiveness, truly loves God. . . .

Thus, love of God should be our aim. It is the first commandment—the foundation of faith. As we develop love of God and Christ, love of family and neighbor will naturally follow. . . . Through love of God, the pain caused by the fiery canker of contention will be extinguished from the soul.

JOY IN YOUR JOURNEY

Is any thing too hard for the Lord?

GENESIS 18:14

You can accomplish the impossible. You can help shape the destiny of the entire human family! As you know and apply the teachings of the Lord in your lives and in your work, you can change the world.

You will have moments of dismay. But you should remember that each of you is literally and truly a son or daughter of Almighty God. You have been created in His very image.

Physically, He wants you to honor the body He has given you. He wants you to treasure and care for your body as your own personal temple. Spiritually, He has sent you here to be successful and to have joy in your journey in mortality. He wants each of you to know that "with God nothing shall be impossible" (Luke 1:37).

THE REWARDS
OF OBEDIENCE

If ye be willing and obedient,
ye shall eat the good of the land.

ISAIAH 1:19

You will find true joy in total obedience to God's laws. While some others choose which commandments they will keep, you know the fallacy and danger of this approach. It will only lead to misery. You will gain protection and spiritual strength in complete obedience. After all, he or she who does not stand for something will likely fall for anything. What will keep you joyful and safe, physically and spiritually? Obedience! Obedience to *all* of God's commandments will allow the Holy Ghost to be your constant companion. Obedience to your baptismal covenants, renewed weekly as you partake of the sacrament, will allow the Spirit of the Lord to be with you. Such obedience will prepare you to be great leaders, great wives and husbands, great mothers and fathers. Such obedience will allow you to become more like the Lord.

LOVE AS HE LOVED

Therefore, what manner of men ought ye to be?
Verily I say unto you, even as I am.

3 NEPHI 27:27

Jesus Christ's exemplary life was His ministry in mortality. He taught us how to live, how to love, how to pray, how to focus on His ordinances, how to know and teach His scriptures, and how to follow His example and endure to the end and more. Enduring to the end includes the endowment of the temple, along with those sealing ordinances that will enable us to return to dwell with Him, and with our Father in Heaven, and with our families.

His ministry among men served to provide an example for us. There is no limit to the number of people who can follow His example. We can love as He loved, we can pray as He prayed, we can focus on the ordinances as He did, we can teach from the scriptures, and we can endure to the end, as He did.

THE DIVINE COVENANT

For of him unto whom much is given much is required; and he who sins against the greater light shall receive the greater condemnation.

DOCTRINE AND COVENANTS 82:3

In the temple we make covenants not only with one another but with God. He fixes the terms, which we are free to accept. He offers principles and ordinances, which we receive by covenant. This places each of us under strong obligation and responsibility to honor that commitment. You need not fear such a pledge, however, because it is never a sacrifice on your part or on mine. Quite to the contrary. Obedience to a divine covenant qualifies us for great blessings and joy beyond our current comprehension.

THE WORK FOR REVELATION

Behold, I have fasted and prayed many days that I might know these things of myself. And now I do know of myself that they are true; for the Lord God hath made them manifest unto me by his Holy Spirit; and this is the spirit of revelation which is in me.

ALMA 5:46

I urge you to stretch beyond your current spiritual ability to receive personal revelation. . . . Nothing opens the heavens quite like the combination of increased purity, exact obedience, earnest seeking, daily feasting on the words of Jesus Christ in the Book of Mormon (see 2 Nephi 32:3), and regular time committed to temple and family history work.

To be sure, there may be times when you feel as though the heavens are closed. But I promise that as you continue to be obedient, expressing gratitude for every blessing the Lord gives you, and as you patiently honor the Lord's timetable, you will be given the knowledge and understanding you seek. Every blessing the Lord has for you—even miracles—will follow. That is what personal revelation will do for you.

WRONG IS
NEVER RIGHT

Woe unto them that call evil good, and good evil;
that put darkness for light, and light for darkness.

ISAIAH 5:20

The temptation to be popular may prioritize public opinion above the word of God. Political campaigns and marketing strategies widely employ public opinion polls to shape their plans. Results of those polls are informative. *But* they could hardly be used as grounds to justify disobedience to God's commandments! Even if "everyone is doing it," wrong is never right. Evil, error, and darkness will never be truth, even if popular. . . .

After World War I, a rather risqué song became popular. In promoting immorality, it vowed that fifty million people cannot be wrong. But in fact, fifty million people *can* be wrong—totally wrong. Immorality is still immorality in the eyes of God, who one day will judge all of our deeds and desires.

FAITH, HOPE, AND CHARITY

And now abideth faith, hope, charity,
these three; but the greatest of these is charity.

1 CORINTHIANS 13:13

Have you noticed in the scriptures that hope seldom stands alone? Hope is often linked with faith. Hope and faith are commonly connected to charity. Why? Because hope is essential to faith; faith is essential to hope; faith and hope are essential to charity. They support one another like legs on a three-legged stool. All three relate to our Redeemer.

Faith is rooted in Jesus Christ. *Hope* centers in his Atonement. *Charity* is manifest in the "pure love of Christ" (Moroni 7:47). These three attributes are intertwined like strands in a cable and may not always be precisely distinguished. Together they become our tether to the celestial kingdom.

OUR IMMORTAL EXISTENCE

Now behold, it was not expedient that man should be reclaimed from this temporal death, for that would destroy the great plan of happiness.

ALMA 42:8

Why do we need such resilient faith? Because difficult days are ahead. Rarely in the future will it be easy or popular to be a faithful Latter-day Saint. Each of us will be tested. The Apostle Paul warned that in the latter days, those who diligently follow the Lord "shall suffer persecution" (2 Timothy 3:12). That very persecution can either crush you into silent weakness or motivate you to be more exemplary and courageous in your daily lives.

A MAGNIFICENT CREATION

In the image of his own body, male and female, created
he them, and blessed them, and called their name
Adam, in the day when they were created and became
living souls in the land upon the footstool of God.

MOSES 6:9

The marvel of our physical bodies is often overlooked. Who has not encountered feelings of low self-esteem because of physique or appearance? Many people wish their bodies could be more to their liking. Some with naturally straight hair want it curly. Others with curly hair want it straight. . . .

Your body, whatever its natural gifts, is a magnificent creation of God. It is a tabernacle of flesh—a temple for your spirit.

THE GREATEST CHOICE

*For thus saith the scripture: Choose ye
this day, whom ye will serve.*

ALMA 30:8

God wants His children to return to Him. But the amazing thing is He allows them to *choose* that course; He doesn't force them. He sends His children to earth, causing a veil of forgetfulness to come upon them. They are here to gain a body, to be tested, and to make choices. The greatest of all choices they may make is to *choose* to return to their Father.

OPTIMISTIC FOR
THE FUTURE

The hope of the righteous shall be gladness.

PROVERBS 10:28

I remain optimistic for the future. I know the great and marvelous blessings that God has in store for those who love Him and serve Him. I see evidence of His hand in this holy work in so many ways. So, during these uncertain times, be comforted by this promise from the Savior. He said, "I, the Lord, am bound when ye do what I say" (Doctrine and Covenants 82:10). I promise you that joy is always within the reach of everyone who will hear Him and obey His laws.

DISPELLING FALSE BELIEFS

And righteousness will I send down out of heaven;
and truth will I send forth out of the earth, to bear
testimony of mine Only Begotten; . . . and truth
will I cause to sweep the earth as with a flood.

MOSES 7:62

The Book of Mormon both illuminates the teachings of the Master and exposes the tactics of the adversary. The Book of Mormon teaches true doctrine to dispel false religious traditions—such as the erroneous practice of performing infant baptisms. The Book of Mormon gives purpose to life by urging us to ponder the potential of eternal life and "never-ending happiness" (Mosiah 2:41). The Book of Mormon shatters the false beliefs that happiness can be found in wickedness and that individual goodness is all that is required to return to the presence of God. It abolishes forever the false concepts that revelation ended with the Bible and that the heavens are sealed today.

MARCH

And whatsoever thing persuadeth
men to do good is of me; for good
cometh of none save it be of me. I am
the same that leadeth men to all good;
he that will not believe my words will
not believe me—that I am; and he that
will not believe me will not believe
the Father who sent me. For behold,
I am the Father, I am the light, and
the life, and the truth of the world.

ETHER 4:12

WORTHY OF THE TEMPLE

*The Prophet Elijah was to plant in the hearts of the children
the promises made to their fathers, foreshadowing the great
work to be done in the temples of the Lord in the dispensation
of the fulness of times, for the redemption of the dead, and the
sealing of the children to their parents, lest the whole earth
be smitten with a curse and utterly wasted at his coming.*

DOCTRINE AND COVENANTS 138:47–48

Families are to be sealed together for all eternity. A
welding link is to be forged between the fathers and the
children. In our time, a whole, complete, and perfect
union of all dispensations, keys, and powers are to be
welded together. For these sacred purposes, holy temples
now dot the earth. I emphasize again that construction
of these temples may not change your life, but your service in the temple surely will.

The time is coming when those who do not obey the
Lord will be separated from those who do. Our safest in-
surance is to continue to be worthy of admission to His
holy house. The greatest gift you could give to the Lord
is to keep yourself unspotted from the world, worthy to
attend His holy house. His gift to you will be the peace
and security of knowing that you are worthy to meet
Him, whenever that time comes.

GOD'S AGENTS

And, ye fathers, provoke not your children to wrath: but bring them up in the nurture and admonition of the Lord.

EPHESIANS 6:4

When a child needs correction, you might ask yourself, "What can I say or do that would persuade him or her to choose a better way?" When giving necessary correction, do it quietly, privately, lovingly, and not publicly. If a rebuke is required, show an increase of love promptly so that seeds of resentment may not remain. To be persuasive, your love must be sincere and your teachings based on divine doctrine and correct principles.

Do not try to control your children. Instead, listen to them, help them to learn the gospel, inspire them, and lead them toward eternal life. You are God's agents in the care of children He has entrusted to you. Let His divine influence remain in your hearts as you teach and persuade.

CHILDREN OF GOD'S BATTALION

But ye are a chosen generation, a royal priesthood, an holy nation,
a peculiar people; that ye should shew forth the praises of him
who hath called you out of darkness into his marvellous light.

1 PETER 2:9

You are sons and daughters of God. You already know this. You have sung about it since you were toddlers. But let me clarify a distinguishing characteristic about *your* identity. You are the children whom God chose to be part of His battalion during this great climax in the longstanding battle between good and evil—between truth and error. I would not be surprised if, when the veil is lifted in the next life, we learn that you actually pled with our Heavenly Father to be reserved for now. I would not be surprised to learn that premortally, you loved the Lord so much that you promised to defend His name and gospel during this world's tumultuous winding-up scenes. One thing is certain: You are of the House of Israel and you have been sent here to help gather God's elect.

SELF-MASTERY

All men that are in a state of nature, or I would say, in a carnal state, are in the gall of bitterness and in the bonds of iniquity; they are without God in the world, and they have gone contrary to the nature of God; therefore, they are in a state contrary to the nature of happiness.

ALMA 41:11

A pivotal spiritual attribute is that of self-mastery— the strength to place reason over appetite. Self-mastery builds a strong conscience. And your conscience determines your moral responses in difficult, tempting, and trying situations. Fasting helps your spirit to develop dominance over your physical appetites. Fasting also increases your access to heaven's help, as it intensifies your prayers. Why the need for self-mastery? God implanted strong appetites within us for nourishment and love, vital for the human family to be perpetuated. When we master our appetites within the bounds of God's laws, we can enjoy longer life, greater love, and consummate joy.

GATHERING AND THE BOOK OF MORMON

The words of your seed should proceed forth out of my mouth unto your seed; and my words shall hiss forth unto the ends of the earth, for a standard unto my people, which are of the house of Israel.

2 NEPHI 29:2

The coming forth of the Book of Mormon is a sign to the entire world that the Lord has commenced to gather Israel and fulfill the covenants He made to Abraham, Isaac, and Jacob. The Book of Mormon declares the doctrine of the gathering (see, for example, 1 Nephi 10:14). It causes people to learn about Jesus Christ, to believe His gospel, and to join His Church. In fact, if there were no Book of Mormon, the promised gathering of Israel would not occur.

Missionary work is also crucial to that gathering. Servants of the Lord go forth proclaiming the Restoration. In many nations our members and missionaries have searched for those of scattered Israel.

MINISTERING IN
THE LORD'S NAME

Whosoever will be great among you,
let him be your minister.

MATTHEW 20:26

A hallmark of the Lord's true and living Church will always be an organized, directed effort to minister to individual children of God and their families. Because it is His Church, we as His servants will minister to the one, just as He did. We will minister in His name, with His power and authority, and with His loving-kindness.

REACHING UP

And they that know thy name will put their trust in thee:
for thou, Lord, hast not forsaken them that seek thee.

PSALM 9:10

Do you remember the biblical story of the woman who suffered for twelve years with a debilitating problem? She exercised great faith in the Savior, exclaiming, "If I may touch but his clothes, I shall be whole" (Mark 5:28). This faithful, focused woman needed to stretch as far as she could to access His power. Her physical stretching was symbolic of her spiritual stretching. . . .

When you reach up for the Lord's power in your life with the same intensity that a drowning person has when grasping and gasping for air, power from Jesus Christ will be yours. When the Savior knows you truly want to reach up to Him—when He can feel that the greatest desire of your heart is to draw His power into your life—you will be led by the Holy Ghost to know exactly what you should do.

NEWSWORTHY
EVENTS

*And behold, I tell you these things that ye may learn wisdom;
that ye may learn that when ye are in the service of your
fellow beings ye are only in the service of your God.*

MOSIAH 2:17

Reports in the media describe newsworthy events. But the truly good deeds—the small, everyday actions of ordinary life—generally go unreported. Noteworthy examples are the employee who gives an honest day's work, the employer who rewards loyalty and service, and the Samaritan who stops to help someone in need. They include the hiker who carries out his own trash and the craftsman who works with a sense of enduring creation. Especially praiseworthy are the man who accepts responsibility for the children he has fathered, the father who wants the respect of his children more than worldly acclaim, and the mother who nurtures an infant as a sacred trust and not as a second-class chore.

DECISIONS
FOR ETERNITY

Cheer up your hearts, and remember that ye are free to act for yourselves—to choose the way of everlasting death or the way of eternal life.

2 NEPHI 10:23

The wise use of your freedom to make your own decisions is crucial to your spiritual growth, now and for eternity. You are never too young to learn, never too old to change. Your yearnings to learn and change come from a divinely instilled striving for eternal progression. Each day brings opportunity for decisions for eternity.

BEGIN WITH
THE END

Seek ye first the kingdom of God, and his righteousness;
and all these things shall be added unto you.

MATTHEW 6:33

In your important race, I would plead for you to begin with the end in mind. To assist you in defining that end, I would ask you this simple question: What would you like said about you at your funeral? Or, if you were to write your own eulogy and you could have only three sentences (no big flowery speeches, please), what would you want to say?

If it's fair for me to ask that of you, it's fair for you to ask that of me. If I were to write what I hope might be said about me, those three sentences would include:

I was able to render service of worth to my fellowmen.

I had a fine family.

I evidenced unshakable faith in God and lived accordingly.

THE PRIVILEGE OF
REVELATION

*And to them will I reveal all mysteries, yea, all the hidden
mysteries of my kingdom from days of old, and for ages to
come, will I make known unto them the good pleasure of
my will concerning all things pertaining to my kingdom.*

DOCTRINE AND COVENANTS 76:7

The privilege of receiving revelation is one of the greatest gifts of God to His children. Through the manifestations of the Holy Ghost, the Lord will assist us in all our righteous pursuits. I remember in an operating room, I have stood over a patient—unsure how to perform an unprecedented procedure—and experienced the Holy Ghost diagramming the technique in my mind. . . .

Imagine the miracle of it! Whatever our Church calling, we can pray to our Heavenly Father and receive guidance and direction, be warned about dangers and distractions, and be enabled to accomplish things we simply could not do on our own. If we will truly receive the Holy Ghost and learn to discern and understand His promptings, we will be guided in matters large and small.

TRULY CONVERTED

All those who humble themselves before God, and desire to be baptized, and come forth with broken hearts and contrite spirits, and witness before the church that they have truly repented of all their sins, and are willing to take upon them the name of Jesus Christ . . . shall be received by baptism into his church.

DOCTRINE AND COVENANTS 20:37

As true converts, we are motivated to do what the Lord wants us to do and to be who He wants us to be. The remission of sins, which brings divine forgiveness, heals the spirit.

How do we know if we are truly converted? Self-examination tests are available in the scriptures. One measures the degree of conversion prerequisite to baptism. Another measures our willingness to serve others. . . . Willingness to serve and strengthen others stands as a symbol of one's readiness to be healed.

THE QUEST FOR KNOWLEDGE

*For the law was given by Moses, but grace
and truth came by Jesus Christ.*

JOHN 1:17

The quest for knowledge is endless. It seems that the more we know, the more there is yet to learn. It is impossible that man may learn all the ways of God. But as we are faithful and are deeply rooted in scriptural accounts of God's magnificent creations, we will be well prepared for future discoveries. All truth is compatible because it all emanates from God.

A WAY BACK

*Repent, and turn yourselves from all your
transgressions; so iniquity shall not be your ruin.*

EZEKIEL 18:30

There *is always* a way back. Jesus Christ (and His gospel) is the way. You have not committed any sin so serious that you are beyond the reach of the Savior's love and atoning grace. As you take steps to repent and follow God's laws, you will begin to feel just how much Heavenly Father and His Beloved Son want you back home with Them! They want you to be happy. They will do anything within Their power that does not violate *your* agency or *Their* laws to help you come back. How I cherish the privilege of feeling Their love for you!

THE RIVER JORDAN

Except a man be born of water and of the Spirit,
he cannot enter into the kingdom of God.

JOHN 3:5

To us, the River Jordan is a sacred stream. The Jordan marked the termination of the wandering of the children of Israel. They had journeyed there from the banks of the Nile. Joshua had led some 600,000 Israelite warriors and their families across that roiling River Jordan during flood season, when the waters were suddenly stopped and heaped up to allow the faithful Israelites, carrying the ark of the covenant, to cross an empty river bed.

. . . The baptism [of Jesus Christ] took place in the vicinity of Bethabara. *Bethabara* in Hebrew means "house of the crossing." . . . Could it be that Jesus Christ chose this location for His baptism in the River Jordan as a silent commemoration of the crossing of those faithful Israelites under Joshua's direction so many years before, as well as a symbol that baptism is a spiritual crossing into the kingdom of God?

COME UNTO HIM

For even hereunto were ye called: because Christ also suffered for us, leaving us an example, that ye should follow his steps.

1 PETER 2:21

Whoever you are and wherever you go, I invite you to come to the outstretched arms of Jesus. Wherever else you think you may be going, come unto Him first. You will find your greatest success and happiness when yoked with Him. In His love, your precious families can be linked together forever, according to the eternal ordinances and covenants that He has established. I invite you to learn of Him, to follow Him, and love Him as I do.

I know of no other way for you to find true happiness. Sometimes we try to come unto Him too tangentially, with a focus on meetings, activities, or procedures. Important as they may be, we should strive to emulate His example and develop a deep understanding of and gratitude for His Atonement. Only as we know the divine attributes of the Father and of the Son can we gain enduring faith in them.

COVENANT-KEEPING WOMEN

*And Ruth said, Entreat me not to leave thee, or to
return from following after thee: for whither thou goest,
I will go; and where thou lodgest, I will lodge:
thy people shall be my people, and thy God my God.*

RUTH 1:16

My dear sisters, nothing is more crucial to your eternal life than your own conversion. It is converted, covenant-keeping women . . . whose righteous lives will increasingly stand out in a deteriorating world and who will thus be seen as different and distinct in the *happiest* of ways.

So today I plead with my sisters of The Church of Jesus Christ of Latter-day Saints to step forward! Take your rightful and needful place in your home, in your community, and in the kingdom of God—more than you ever have before. I plead with you to fulfill President Kimball's prophecy [to reflect righteousness] (*Teachings of Presidents of the Church: Spencer W. Kimball* [2006], 222–23). And I promise you in the name of Jesus Christ that as you do so, the Holy Ghost will magnify your influence in an unprecedented way!

THE DESIGN
OF A TEMPLE

*Behold, I give unto you power, that whatsoever ye shall
seal on earth shall be sealed in heaven; and whatsoever
ye shall loose on earth shall be loosed in heaven; and
thus shall ye have power among this people.*

HELAMAN 10:7

The design of a temple is functional. Every element in
the architecture and atmosphere of the temple contributes to its function, which is to teach and to bless. The
temple teaches of Jesus Christ. The endowment comprises
a course of instruction relating to the eternal journey of a
man and woman from their premortal existence through
the earthly experience and on to the exaltation that each
may attain. The temple blesses with ordinances and instructions of the Lord. It blesses with the ultimate linkage in God's plan of happiness to unite families forever.

FACE THE FUTURE
WITH OPTIMISM

This is the day which the Lord hath made;
we will rejoice and be glad in it.

PSALM 118:24

We live in the most vibrant era in the history of the world. I wake up every morning eager for the adventures of the day. And I hope you feel that same exuberance for the gift of life. Though our world is filled with serious challenges, I am optimistic about the future and confident about the fundamental goodness of humankind. I marvel at the compassionate outreach we see constantly from the leaders and members of other faiths and from people of goodwill everywhere who seek to reduce human suffering wherever it is found. . . . I give you my assurance that regardless of the world's condition and your personal circumstances, you can face the future with optimism and joy—if you have faith in the Lord Jesus Christ and His gospel.

PEACE IN JESUS CHRIST

For he is our peace, who hath made both one, and hath broken down the middle wall of partition between us.

EPHESIANS 2:14

Jesus Christ can bring peace to those whose lives have been ravaged by war. Families disrupted by military duty bear memories of war, which in my mind were imbedded during the Korean War. Wars of our present era are more sophisticated but are still as wrenching to families. Those who so suffer can turn to the Lord. His is the consoling message of peace on earth and good will among men (see Luke 2:14). . . .

Peace can come to all who earnestly seek the Prince of Peace. His is the sweet and saving message our missionaries take throughout the world.

WHAT A BLESSING!

*And this shall ye do in remembrance of my body, which I
have shown unto you. And it shall be a testimony unto the
Father that ye do always remember me. And if ye do always
remember me ye shall have my Spirit to be with you.*

3 NEPHI 18:7

Partake of the sacrament regularly. Partake of the
bread, broken in remembrance of the body of the Son of
God. Drink the water in remembrance of His precious
blood that was shed for us.

Witness unto God, the Eternal Father, that you are
willing to take upon yourself the name of His Son and
always remember Him and keep His commandments
which He has given you. If you will do this, you may
always have the Spirit to be with you. What a blessing!

ENDURANCE THROUGH TRIALS

And ye shall be hated of all men for my name's sake:
but he that endureth to the end shall be saved.

MATTHEW 10:22

Be we reminded that the Father did not deliver His Son from grief by removing the trial. He allowed the Son to finish the mission He came to perform. The Son was given the ability to endure to the end.

So each of us, in order to endure [any] trial, will need to couple forgiveness with faith, humility with righteousness. The Savior's Atonement and Resurrection gave Him the power to deliver each of us from grief. He really knows how you feel—each one of you.

DIVINE BLESSINGS, DIVINE LAW

Then Peter and the other apostles answered and said,
We ought to obey God rather than men.

ACTS 5:29

While nominally I come to you from the science of surgery and its mother of medicine, in a truer sense, I have been forged from the stern discipline of law—not the laws of men, as mastered by our brethren of the legal profession, but the eternal and unchanging laws of our Divine Creator.

The surgeon soon learns the incontrovertibility of divine law. He knows that hopes and wishes are sometimes simply powerless sham. Desired blessings come only be obedience to divine law, and in no other way. . . . Only as the laws are known, and then obeyed, can the blessings we desire by earned. . . . The endless laws of the Lord are the doctrines taught by His Apostles.

ONE HEART AND
ONE MIND

Be ye all of one mind, having compassion one of another, love as brethren, be pitiful, be courteous.

1 PETER 3:8

In a . . . prayer, Jesus included a plea for unity. "Father," He said, "I pray unto thee for them, . . . that they may believe in me, that I may be in them as thou, Father, art in me, that we may be one" (3 Nephi 19:23). We too can pray for unity. We can pray to be of one heart and one mind with the Lord's anointed and with our loved ones. We can pray for mutual understanding and respect between ourselves and our neighbors. If we really care for others, we should pray for them.

THE DIVINE
CREATION

*Behold, all these are kingdoms, and any man
who hath seen any or the least of these hath seen
God moving in his majesty and power.*

DOCTRINE AND COVENANTS 88:47

I testify that the earth and all life upon it are of divine origin. The Creation did not happen by chance. It did not come *ex nihilo* (out of nothing). And human minds and hands able to build buildings or create computers are not accidental. It is God who made us and not we ourselves. We are His people! The Creation itself testifies of a Creator. We cannot disregard the divine in the Creation. Without our grateful awareness of God's hand in the Creation, we would be just as oblivious to our provider as are goldfish swimming in a bowl. With deep gratitude, we echo the words of the Psalmist, who said, "O Lord, how manifold are thy works! in wisdom hast though made them all: the earth is full of thy riches" (Psalm 104:24).

HEAVENLY HELP

The preparations of the heart in man, and the
answer of the tongue, is from the Lord.

PROVERBS 16:1

More amazing than modern technology is our opportunity to access information directly from heaven,
without hardware, software, or monthly service fees. It
is one of the most marvelous gifts the Lord has offered to
mortals. It is His generous invitation to "*ask,* and it shall
be given you; *seek,* and ye shall find; *knock,* and it shall be
opened unto you" (Matthew 7:7).

[God's] timeless offer to provide personal revelation
is extended to all of His children. It almost sounds too
good to be true. But it is true! I have received and re-
sponded to that heavenly help. And I have learned that I
always need to be ready to receive it.

JESUS CHRIST'S MISSION

And he will take upon him death, that he may loose the bands
of death which bind his people; and he will take upon him
their infirmities, that his bowels may be filled with mercy,
according to the flesh, that he may know according to the
flesh how to succor his people according to their infirmities.

ALMA 7:12

Jesus Christ's mission was the Atonement. That mission was uniquely His. Born of a mortal mother and an immortal Father, He was the only one who could voluntarily lay down His life and take it up again (see John 10:14–18). The glorious consequences of His Atonement were infinite and eternal. He took the sting out of death and made temporary the grief of the grave. His responsibility for the Atonement was known even before the Creation and the Fall. Not only was it to provide for the resurrection and immortality of all humankind, but it was also to enable us to be forgiven of our sins—upon conditions established by Him. Thus His Atonement opened the way by which we could be united with Him and with our families eternally. This prospect we esteem as eternal life—the greatest gift of God to man.

A DELIGHTFUL SABBATH

*If thou turn away . . . from doing thy pleasure on my holy
day; and call the sabbath a delight, the holy of the Lord,
honourable; and shalt honour him, not doing thine own
ways, nor finding thine own pleasure, nor speaking thine
own words: Then shalt thou delight thyself in the Lord.*

ISAIAH 58:13–14

Not pursuing your "own pleasure" on the Sabbath requires self-discipline (see Isaiah 58:13). You may have to
deny yourself of something you might like. If you choose
to delight yourself *in the Lord,* you will not permit yourself to treat it as any other day. Routine and recreational
activities can be done some other time.

Think of this: In paying tithing, we return one-tenth
of our increase to the Lord. In keeping the Sabbath holy,
we reserve one day in seven as His. So it is our privilege
to consecrate both money and time to Him who lends
us life each day.

Faith in God engenders a love for the Sabbath; faith in
the Sabbath engenders a love for God. A sacred Sabbath
truly is a delight.

THE POWER OF MUSIC

*If thou art merry, praise the Lord with singing, with music,
with dancing, and with a prayer of praise and thanksgiving.*

DOCTRINE AND COVENANTS 136:28

Worthy music is not only a source of power but also of protection. . . . Wherever we are we should carefully choose what we see and hear. We would not knowingly tolerate pornography in our homes, but if we are not careful, we may allow music into our lives that can be just as devastating. . . .

As you know, continued exposure to loud sounds will, in time, damage delicate organs of hearing. In like manner, if you overindulge in loud music, you will more likely become spiritually deaf, unable to hear the still, small voice. . . .

Do not allow unworthy, raucous music to enter your life. It is *not* harmless. It can weaken your defense and allow unworthy thoughts into your mind and pave the way to unworthy acts.

GIVE THE LORD TIME

And now, Israel, what doth the Lord thy God require
of thee, but to fear the Lord thy God, to walk in all
his ways, and to love him, and to serve the Lord thy
God with all thy heart and with all thy soul.

DEUTERONOMY 10:12

Spend more time—much more time—in places where
the Spirit is present. That means more time with friends
who are seeking to have the Spirit with them. Spend
more time on your knees in prayer, more time in the
scriptures, more time in family history work, more time
in the temple. I promise you that as you consistently
give the Lord a generous portion of your time, He will
multiply the remainder.

PRIESTHOOD POWER

*And Stephen, full of faith and power, did great
wonders and miracles among the people.*

ACTS 6:8

In these latter days, we know there will be earthquakes in diverse places. Perhaps one of those diverse places will be in our own homes, where emotional, financial, or spiritual "earthquakes" may occur. Priesthood power can calm the seas and heal fractures in the earth. Priesthood power can also calm the minds and heal fractures in the hearts of those we love.

Are we willing to pray, fast, study, seek, worship, and serve as men of God so we can have that kind of priesthood power?

APRIL

And it came to pass that the Lord
spake unto them saying: Arise and
come forth unto me, that ye may thrust
your hands into my side, and also that
ye may feel the prints of the nails in
my hands and in my feet, that ye may
know that I am the God of Israel, and
the God of the whole earth, and have
been slain for the sins of the world.

3 NEPHI 11:13–14

HEED HIS PROPHETS

Now therefore ye are no more strangers and foreigners,
but fellowcitizens with the saints, and of the household of
God; and are built upon the foundation of the apostles and
prophets, Jesus Christ himself being the chief corner stone.

EPHESIANS 2:19–20

If the most important things in life are to know God and to keep His commandments, then to heed His prophets and abide by their teachings should be among our most important educational objectives. In a way, the very repetition of the teachings of prophets may have sounded monotonous through the years. The pleadings of Abraham, Isaac, Jacob, Moses, and Abinadi have not differed significantly from those of [today's prophets]. Surely, when measured by eternal standards, teachings of the prophets are more important and enduring than the latest findings of competent researchers, even if these findings were both discovered and taught by use of modern technology and teaching aids.

BE LIKE JESUS CHRIST

With my whole heart have I sought thee:
O let me not wander from thy commandments.

PSALM 119:10

When priorities are proper, the power to endure is increased. And when internalized, those priorities will help keep you from "going overboard." They will protect you from cheating—in marriage, in the Church, and in life.

If you really want to *be* like the Lord—more than any *thing* or *anyone* else—you will remember that your adoration of Jesus is best shown by your emulation of Him. Then you will not allow any other love to become more important than love for your companion, your family, and your Creator. You will govern yourself not by someone else's set of rules but by revealed principles of truth.

PERFECT BALANCE

Thus speaketh the Lord of hosts, saying, Execute true judgment,
and shew mercy and compassions every man to his brother.
ZECHARIAH 7:9

An erroneous assumption could be made that if a little of something is good, a lot must be better. Not so! Overdoses of needed medication can be toxic. Boundless mercy could oppose justice. So tolerance, without limit, could lead to spineless permissiveness.

The Lord drew boundary lines to define acceptable limits of tolerance. Danger rises when those divine limits are disobeyed. Just as parents teach little children not to run and play in the street, the Savior taught us that we need not tolerate evil.

LOVE LIFE

*For our light affliction, which is but for a moment, worketh
for us a far more exceeding and eternal weight of glory.*

2 CORINTHIANS 4:17

As a special witness of Jesus Christ, I testify that He
lives! I also testify that the veil of death is very thin.
I know by experiences too sacred to relate that those
who have gone before are not strangers to leaders of this
Church. To us and to you, our loved ones may be just
as close as the next room—separated only by the doors
of death.

With that assurance, brothers and sisters, love life!
Cherish each moment as a blessing from God. Live it
well—even to your loftiest potential. Then the anticipa-
tion of death shall not hold you hostage.

FEED MY SHEEP

He saith unto him the third time, Simon, son of Jonas, lovest thou me? Peter was grieved because he said unto him the third time, Lovest thou me? And he said unto him, Lord, thou knowest all things; thou knowest that I love thee. Jesus saith unto him, Feed my sheep.

JOHN 21:17

As we embark in this new responsibility we have for ministering, we are to be ministers among our fellow-men. How are you going to do that? Just the way Jesus did, that's all.

Find someone who is having a bad day, who has had some bad news, or who is lonely or afraid, feeling unwanted or unloved. Take care of them. . . . We can become physicians, in a way—spiritual physicians. We may have to diagnose what the problem is, where the pain is coming from, but no matter what it is, the gospel of Jesus Christ has within it the power to lift and to love, to serve. That is all we are asking—just minister.

THE JOYFUL RESTORATION

Now, what do we hear in the gospel which we have received?
A voice of gladness! A voice of mercy from heaven; and a
voice of truth out of the earth. . . . How beautiful upon the
mountains are the feet of those that bring glad tidings of good
things, and that say unto Zion: behold, they God reigneth!

DOCTRINE AND COVENANTS 128:19

God the Father and His Beloved Son, Jesus Christ, appeared to Joseph Smith in a vision. That singular event in human history initiated the Restoration of the Lord's gospel—an unfolding Restoration that continues today.

God loves all of His children and has a vision for each of us. Just as He listened to Joseph's prayer in 1820, He listens to you and yearns to speak with you through the Spirit. We invite you to be a major part of sharing the message of the ongoing restoration of the Savior's gospel.

WORLDLY DISTRACTIONS

*Behold, the world is ripening in iniquity; and it must
needs be that the children of men are stirred up unto
repentance, both the Gentiles and also the house of Israel.*

DOCTRINE AND COVENANTS 18:6

Sometimes we speak almost casually about walking away from the world with its contention, pervasive temptations, and false philosophies. But *truly* doing so requires you to examine your life meticulously and regularly. As you do so, the Holy Ghost will prompt you about what is no longer needful, what is no longer worthy of your time and energy.

As you shift your focus away from worldly distractions, some things that seem important to you now will recede in priority. You will need to say no to some things, even though they may seem harmless. As you embark upon and continue this lifelong process of consecrating your life to the Lord, the changes in your perspective, feelings, and spiritual strength will amaze you!

PROCLAIM THE GOOD NEWS

Therefore, verily I say unto you, lift up your voices unto this people; speak the thoughts that I shall put into your hearts, and you shall not be confounded before men; for it shall be given you in the very hour, yea, in the very moment, what ye shall say.

DOCTRINE AND COVENANTS 100:5–6

The Lord cannot proclaim His good news of salvation through silent servants. Often you will need to be daringly declarative. There may be times, however, when you need to be courageously quiet. If you are connected well with the Lord, you will know how to respond. Think as He would. Do as He would. "Feast upon the words of Christ. . . . [His words] will tell you all things what you should do" (2 Nephi 32:3).

LOVING
THE SCRIPTURES

*I speak the same words unto one nation like unto another. And
when the two nations shall run together the testimony of the two
nations shall run together also. And I do this that I may prove
unto many that I am the same yesterday, today, and forever.*

2 NEPHI 29:8–9

Love for the Book of Mormon expands one's love for
the Bible and vice versa. Scriptures of the Restoration
do not compete with the Bible; they complement the
Bible. We are indebted to martyrs who gave their lives
so that we could have the Bible. It establishes the everlasting nature of the gospel and of the plan of happiness.
The Book of Mormon restores and underscores biblical
teachings such as tithing, the temple, the Sabbath day,
and the priesthood.

An angel proclaimed that the Book of Mormon shall
establish the truth of the Bible. He also revealed that
writings in the Bible available in our day are not as complete as they were when originally written by prophets
and apostles. He declared that the Book of Mormon
shall restore plain and precious things taken away from
the Bible.

LIGHT AND LIFE

Jesus answered and said unto her, Whosoever drinketh of this water shall thirst again: But whosoever drinketh of the water that I shall give him shall never thirst; but the water that I shall give him shall be in him a well of water springing up into everlasting life.

JOHN 4:13–14

The modern-day scene in Caesarea Philippi is unique. There is a mountain at the base of which is a mighty rock from which water seems to be flowing. These cascades comprise one of the three major headwaters of the River Jordan, literally the liquid lifeline of that country. As Jesus was preparing to conclude His mortal ministry, here He trained future leaders of His Church. Could it be that the Savior brought His disciples to this spot to teach the lesson that this majestic mountain symbolized the rock of Christ from whom revelation would flow?—revelation to bring light and life to them.

RELIGIOUS FREEDOM

We claim the privilege of worshiping Almighty God according to the dictates of our own conscience, and allow all men the same privilege, let them worship how, where, or what they may.

ARTICLES OF FAITH 1:11

Man's unending search for happiness will ever include a quest for truth, and that needs freedom to flourish. That means freedom to change one's mind—even to change one's religion—in response to new information and inspiration. Freedom to change one's religion is a fundamental human right. After all, one's religion is not imposed by others. It is not predetermined, either by parentage or geography. It is a very personal and sacred choice, nestled at the very core of human dignity. . . .

Freedom of religious expression is something not to be feared. It will produce finer individuals, changed for good. Their families will be stronger and more secure. They will be better citizens who honor the laws of the land, who are more charitable, more peaceful and prosperous.

TEMPLES OF GOD

Know ye not that ye are the temple of God,
and that the Spirit of God dwelleth in you?

1 CORINTHIANS 3:16

In a very real sense, each of us stands as a temple of God. Your personal temple is a gift from God. It is holy. Please protect it as such. The fact that your body is a sacred sanctuary is also known by Satan. He, who has no body, would like you to deface and defile yours.

YOUR HIGHEST PRIORITY

*And, if you keep my commandments and endure
to the end you shall have eternal life, which
gift is the greatest of all the gifts of God.*

DOCTRINE AND COVENANTS 14:7

More than anything else in this world, you want to make choices that lead to the ultimate and glorious destiny of eternal life. That is God's great glory for you. Choose eternal life as your highest priority! Study the scriptures, such as sections 76 and 88 of the Doctrine and Covenants, in order to understand more about the different blessings awaiting those who choose eternal life and those who don't. Choose eternal life as your highest priority, and notice how other choices fall into place.

LABORATORY
OF LOVE

Hereby perceive we the love of God, because he laid down his life for us: and we ought to lay down our lives for the brethren. But whoso hath this world's good, and seeth his brother have need, and shutteth up his bowels of compassion from him, how dwelleth the love of God in him?

1 JOHN 3:16–17

Happiness at home is most likely to be achieved when practices there are founded upon the teachings of Jesus Christ. Ours is the responsibility to ensure that we have family prayer, scripture study, and family home evening. Ours is the responsibility to prepare our children to receive the ordinances of salvation and exaltation and the blessings promised to tithe payers. Ours is the privilege to bestow priesthood blessings of healing, comfort, and direction.

The home is the great laboratory of love. There the raw chemicals of selfishness and greed are melded in the crucible of cooperation to yield compassionate concern and love one for another.

HOW THE LORD GOVERNS HIS CHURCH

*For the Lord shall be in their midst, and his glory shall be
upon them, and he will be their king and their lawgiver.*

DOCTRINE AND COVENANTS 45:59

Think about the majestic manner by which the Lord
governs His Church. When a President of the Church
passes away, there is no mystery about who is next called
to serve in that capacity. There is no electioneering, no
campaigning, but only the quiet workings of a divine
plan of succession put in place by the Lord Himself.

Each day of an Apostle's service is a day of learning
and preparing for more responsibility in the future. It
takes decades of service for an Apostle to move from
the junior chair to the senior chair in the circle. During
that time, he gains firsthand experience in each facet of
the work of the Church. . . . This process of succession
in the leadership of the Church is unique. I know of
nothing else like it. That should not surprise us, because
this is the Lord's Church. He does not work after the
manner of men.

SUFFERED
FOR ALL

I, God, have suffered these things for all, that they might not
suffer if they would repent; but if they would not repent they
must suffer even as I; which suffering caused myself, even
God, the greatest of all, to tremble because of pain, and to
bleed at every pore, and to suffer both body and spirit.

DOCTRINE AND COVENANTS 19:16–18

As members of [Jesus Christ's] Church we understand
the deep significance of His Atonement, even though
we cannot completely comprehend the miracle of it. . . .
Each time I reflect upon the ordeal of His Atonement, I
realize that He didn't have to do it. He did it voluntarily.
And for it, He was "despised and rejected of men, a man
of sorrows and acquainted with grief" (Isaiah 53:3).

All who are parents know the heartache felt when
loved ones endure trials. The parents of Jesus were no
exception. It is hard to comprehend the feelings of the
Father who had to withdraw His spirit at His son's last
hour, so that the victory of the Atonement could be
earned completely by Jesus. Yet, meek Jesus gave the
glory to His Father.

STRENGTHENING MARRIAGE

*For where your treasure is,
there will your heart be also.*

MATTHEW 6:21

Family relationships start with the love of a husband for his wife, and of a wife for her husband. Marriage brings two very different and imperfect people together. Husbands and wives deal with their imperfections best with patience and a sense of humor. Each should stand ready to say, "I'm sorry! Please forgive me." And each should be a peacemaker. . . .

Marriage is sanctified by family prayer morning and night, and daily scripture study. Marriage is stabilized by careful financial planning, avoiding debt, and living within a budget with willing obedience to the Lord's law of tithing. Marriage is energized by making prime time together. Marriage is protected by an absolute commitment to make it successful.

UNITY
IN DIVERSITY

Neglect not the gift that is in thee.
1 TIMOTHY 4:14

We can't all do all things. Circumstances, available time, and talents vary widely among us. Your diversities take you to numerous arenas of activity. There let your presence be felt. . . .

You can—you must—make a difference. You are vital to the Lord's team—one team with one purpose. Through your diversity, build strength in unity. Bind yourselves together in all holiness.

SYNERGIZING INTERESTS

Seek not for riches but for wisdom, and behold, the mysteries of God shall be unfolded unto you, and then shall you be made rich. Behold, he that hath eternal life is rich.

DOCTRINE AND COVENANTS 6:7

Some of you have already defined your goals. Some have even developed a system of priorities to give order to your interests and responsibilities. I applaud such discipline and think it's useful, but I believe that this ordering process may often be a little artificial. Rarely do we fragment the life that we live. It is not possible to influence one facet of our life without that affecting other aspects as well. So, in my own experience, I have preferred not to compartmentalize my interests, but to synergize them.

ELECT WOMEN

*Behold, thy sins are forgiven thee, and thou
art an elect lady, whom I have called.*

DOCTRINE AND COVENANTS 25:3

We need women who know how to make important things happen by their faith and who are courageous defenders of morality and families in a sin-sick world. We need women who are devoted to shepherding God's children along the covenant path toward exaltation; women who know how to receive personal revelation; who understand the power and peace of the temple endowment; women who know how to call upon the powers of heaven to protect and strengthen children and families; women who teach fearlessly.

OUR DIVINE NATURE

I have said, Ye are gods; and all of you
are children of the most High.

PSALM 82:6

Above all, teach your children to know and to love God their Heavenly Father. Help them to know that they are created in His image. Each son or daughter is a spirit child of God. Each has a divine nature. Help each one pray to Him—morning and night, at mealtime, and more.

ETERNAL FAMILIES

And I give unto them eternal life; and they shall never perish, neither shall any man pluck them out of my hand.

JOHN 10:28

Are all our sympathies and love for each other only temporary—to be lost in death? No! Can family life endure beyond this period of mortal probation? Yes! God has revealed the eternal nature of celestial marriage and the family as the source our greatest joy.

Material possessions and honors of the world do not endure. But your union as wife, husband, and family can. The only duration of family life that satisfies the loftiest longings of the human soul is forever. No sacrifice is too great to have the blessings of an eternal marriage. To qualify, one needs only to deny oneself of ungodliness and honor the ordinances of the temple. . . . Our family is the focus of our greatest work and joy in this life; so will it be throughout all eternity.

PRAYER IS FREE

As for me, I will call upon God; and the Lord shall save me. Evening, and morning, and at noon, will I pray, and cry aloud: and he shall hear my voice.

PSALM 55:16–17

Through prayer, we can show our love for God. And He has made it so easy. We may pray to Him any time. No special equipment is needed. We don't even need to charge batteries or pay a monthly service fee. . . .

The sweet power of prayer can be intensified by fasting, on occasion, when appropriate to a particular need.

Prayers can be offered even in silence. One can *think* a prayer, especially when words would interfere. We often kneel to pray; we may stand or be seated. Physical position is less important than is spiritual submission to God.

CULTIVATE FRIENDS

Behold, this I have given unto you as a parable, and it is even as I am. I say unto you, be one; and if ye are not one ye are not mine.

DOCTRINE AND COVENANTS 38:27

Cultivate the companionship of good friends. But also seek to broaden your circle. Reach and teach widely, without fear. Enjoy opportunities to learn more from others. Share your testimony often, and be a good friend to all you know. Don't forget to take advantage of choice friendshipping moments with parents, adults, advisers, and bishops. They will welcome your conversation. Surely, silent treatment is beneath the dignity of those who have taken upon themselves the name of Jesus Christ. And play your own part in helping to make your home a place of partnership, prayer, and peace.

BEYOND OUR LIMITS

*But blessed are they who have kept the covenant and
observed the commandment, for they shall obtain mercy.*

DOCTRINE AND COVENANTS 54:6

A covenant made with God is not restrictive, but protective. Such a concept is not new. For example, if our water supply is not clean, we filter the water to screen out harmful ingredients. Divine covenants help us to filter out of our minds impurities that could harm us. When we choose to deny ourselves of all ungodliness, we lose nothing of value and gain the glory of eternal life. Covenants do not hold us down; they elevate us beyond the limits of our own power and perspective.

JESUS'S TITLES

*The woman saith unto him, I know that Messias cometh,
which is called Christ: when he is come, he will tell us all
things. Jesus saith unto her, I that speak unto thee am he.*

JOHN 4:25–26

Jesus was the Anointed One—anointed by Heavenly
Father to be His personal representative in all things pertaining to the salvation of mankind. Jesus was anointed
to be our Savior and Redeemer. Before the world was
formed, Jesus was anointed to make immortality a reality and eternal life a possibility for all of God's children.
Thus, Jesus bore two unique titles: *the Messiah* (Hebrew)
and *the Christ* (Greek)—each meaning "anointed" (see
Bible Dictionary, "Anointed One").

GOD'S INFINITE LOVE

There is neither Jew nor Greek, there is neither bond nor free,
there is neither male nor female: for ye are all one in Christ Jesus.

GALATIANS 3:28

When I think of the love I feel for each member of our family, I sense, to a slight degree, the love that our Heavenly Father bears for His children. . . . We teach that God's love for His children is infinite. Regardless of race, nationality, or gender, He loves all of them. He has done so from the beginning and will continue to do so. He invites all to gain eternal exaltation for their family.

FULNESS OF JOY

*Thou wilt shew me the path of life: in thy presence is fulness
of joy; at thy right hand there are pleasures for evermore.*

PSALM 16:11

Joy is powerful, and focusing on joy brings God's power
into our lives. As in all things, Jesus Christ is our ultimate exemplar, "who for the joy that was set before him
endured the cross" (Hebrews 12:2). Think of that! In order for Him to endure the most excruciating experience
ever endured on earth, our Savior focused on *joy*!

And what was the joy that was set before Him?
Surely it included the joy of cleansing, healing, and
strengthening us; the joy of paying for the sins of all who
would repent; the joy of making it possible for you and
me to return home—clean and worthy—to live with our
Heavenly Parents and families.

THE MEDICINE OF
THE GOSPEL

Blessed is the man that trusteth in the
Lord, and whose hope the Lord is.

JEREMIAH 17:7

In a world beset by crises—among people searching for values that endure—the gospel of Jesus Christ offers hope. It provides immunization from the illness of ignorance. Strength to withstand the wiles of the adversary—resistance to evil's eroding energy—can come from teachings of the Lord. Indeed, spiritual sickness can be precluded by the preventive medicine of the gospel.

NOT WITHOUT HELP

*Counsel with the Lord in all thy doings,
and he will direct thee for good.*

ALMA 37:37

Agency is a divine gift to you. You are free to choose what you will be and what you will do. And you are not without help. Counsel with your parents is a privilege at any age. Prayer provides communication with your Heavenly Father and invites the promptings of personal revelation. And in certain circumstances, consultation with professional advisers and with your local leaders in the Church may be highly advisable, especially when very difficult decisions must be made.

MAY

The scriptures are laid before thee, yea, and all things denote there is a God; yea, even the earth, and all things that are upon the face of it, yea, and its motion, yea, and also all the planets which move in their regular form do witness that there is a Supreme Creator.

ALMA 30:44

A REVERENT SAINT

Wherefore we receiving a kingdom which cannot
be moved, let us have grace, whereby we may serve
God acceptably with reverence and godly fear.

HEBREWS 12:28

Perhaps above all, a saint is reverent. Reverence for the Lord, for the earth He created, for leaders, for the dignity of others, for the law, for the sanctity of life, for chapels and other buildings, are all evidences of saintly attitudes.

A reverent saint loves the Lord and gives highest priority to keeping His commandments. Daily prayer, periodic fasting, payment of tithes and offerings are privileges important to a faithful saint.

FASTING IN JOY

And on this day thou shalt do none other thing, only let thy food be prepared with singleness of heart that thy fasting may be perfect, or, in other words, that thy joy may be full.

DOCTRINE AND COVENANTS 59:13

A step toward self-mastery comes when you . . . observe the law of the fast. As funds are contributed from meals missed, the needs of the poor may be met. But meanwhile, through your spirit, you develop personal power over your body's drives of hunger and thirst. Fasting gives you confidence to know that your spirit can master appetite. . . . Fasting fortifies discipline over appetite and helps to protect against later uncontrolled cravings and gnawing habits.

TRUTH IS TRUTH

Behold, thou knowest that thou hast inquired of me and I did enlighten thy mind; and now I tell thee these things that thou mayest know that thou hast been enlightened by the Spirit of truth.

DOCTRINE AND COVENANTS 6:15

Truth is truth. Some things are simply true. The arbiter of truth is God—not your favorite social media news feed, not Google, and certainly not those who are disaffected from the Church. . . .

Many now claim that truth is relative and that there is no such thing as divine law or a divine plan. Such a claim is simply not true. There *is* a difference between right and wrong. Truth is based upon the laws God has established for the dependability, protection, and nurturing of His children. Eternal laws operate in and affect each of our lives, whether we believe them or not.

THE ONGOING RESTORATION

And the voice of . . . divers angels, from Michael or Adam
down to the present time, all declaring their dispensation,
their rights, their keys, their honors, their majesty and glory,
and the power of their priesthood; giving line upon line,
precept upon precept; . . . giving us consolation by holding
forth that which is to come, confirming our hope!

DOCTRINE AND COVENANTS 128:21

You and I get to participate in the ongoing Restoration of the gospel of Jesus Christ. It is wondrous! It is not man-made! It comes from the Lord. . . . This work is empowered by a divine announcement made 200 years ago. It consisted of only seven words: "This is My Beloved Son. Hear Him!" (Joseph Smith—History 1:17).

Uttered by Almighty God, that announcement brought a young Joseph Smith to the Lord Jesus Christ. Those seven words launched the Restoration of His gospel. Why? Because our living God is a loving God! He wants His children to gain immortality and eternal life! The great latter-day work of which we are a part was established, on schedule, to bless a waiting and weeping world.

MEANS OF CREATION

If ye walk in my statutes, and keep my commandments, and do them; then I will give you rain in due season, and the land shall yield her increase, and the trees of the field shall yield their fruit.

LEVITICUS 26:3–4

The Creation, great as it is, is not an end in itself but a means to an end. We come to the earth for a brief period of time, endure our tests and trials, and prepare to move onward and upward to a glorious homecoming. Our thoughts and deeds while here will surely be more purposeful if we understand God's plan and are thankful for and obedient to His commandments.

A LIVING SACRIFICE

I beseech you therefore, brethren, by the mercies of God, that ye present your bodies a living sacrifice, holy, acceptable unto God, which is your reasonable service.

ROMANS 12:1

Each time you look in the mirror, see your body as your temple. That truth—refreshed gratefully each day—can positively influence your decisions about how you will care for your body and how you will use it. How could this be? Because your body is the temple for your spirit. And how you use your body affects your spirit. Some of the decisions that will determine your eternal destiny include:

How will you choose to care for and use your body?

What spiritual attributes will you choose to develop?

CELESTIAL GLORY

For if you will that I give unto you a place in the celestial world, you must prepare yourselves by doing the things which I have commanded you and required of you.

DOCTRINE AND COVENANTS 78:7

Death is a necessary component of our eternal existence. No one knows when it will come, but it is essential to God's great plan of happiness. Thanks to the Atonement of the Lord, eventual resurrection is a reality and eternal life is a possibility for all humankind. That possibility becomes a reality as we obey God's law. He said, "Except ye shall keep my commandments, . . . ye shall in no case enter into the kingdom of heaven" (3 Nephi 12:20). One day we will be judged by the Lord and go to our own mansion prepared in our Father's heavenly house. Celestial glory awaits those who have been faithful to God's gentle commands.

Brothers and sisters, we live to die and we die to live—in another realm. If we are well prepared, death brings no terror. From an eternal perspective, death is premature only for those who are not prepared to meet God.

BRIGHTER DAYS

For his anger endureth but a moment; in his favour is life:
weeping may endure for a night, but joy cometh in the morning.

PSALM 30:5

Jesus suffered deeply because He loves us deeply! He wants us to repent and be converted so that He can fully heal us.

When sore trials come upon us, it's time to deepen our faith in God, to work hard, and to serve others. Then He will heal our broken hearts. He will bestow upon us personal peace and comfort. Those great gifts will not be destroyed, even by death.

The gift of resurrection is the Lord's consummate act of healing. Thanks to Him, no condition is hopeless. Thanks to Him, brighter days are ahead, both here and hereafter. Real joy awaits each of us—on the other side of sorrow.

HONOR MOTHER, HONOR GOD

He taught me also, and said unto me, Let thine heart retain my words: keep my commandments, and live.

PROVERBS 4:4

If one dishonors the commandments of God, one dishonors mother, and if one dishonors mother, one dishonors the commandments of God. . . .

You can hardly achieve your highest potential without the influence of good women, particularly your mother. . . . Learn now to show respect and gratitude. Remember that your mother is your *mother*. She should not need to issue orders. Her wish, her hope, her hint should provide direction that you would honor. Thank her and express your love for her. . . . The influence of your mother will bless you throughout life.

ALL GOD'S CHILDREN

For behold, the Lord doth grant unto all nations, of their own nation and tongue, to teach his word, yea, in wisdom, all that he seeth fit that they should have; therefore we see that the Lord doth counsel in wisdom, according to that which is just and true.

ALMA 29:8

The Church is the way by which the Master accomplishes His work and bestows His glory. Its ordinances and related covenants are the crowning rewards of our membership. While many organizations can offer fellowship and fine instruction, only His Church can provide baptism, confirmation, ordination, the sacrament, patriarchal blessings, and the ordinances of the temple—all bestowed by authorized priesthood power. That power is destined to bless *all* children of our Heavenly Father, regardless of their nationality.

LOVE AT HOME

Behold, how good and how pleasant it is for
brethren to dwell together in unity!

PSALM 133:1

Individual progression is fostered in the family. . . .
The home is to be God's laboratory of love and service.
There a husband is to love his wife, a wife is to love
her husband, and parents and children are to love one
another. . . .

Our Heavenly Father wants husbands and wives to
be faithful to each other and to esteem and treat their
children as an heritage from the Lord. In such a family
we study the scriptures and pray together. And we fix
our focus on the temple. There we receive the highest
blessings that God has in store for His faithful children.

JESUS CHRIST'S POWER

He giveth power to the faint; and to them that
have no might he increaseth strength.

ISAIAH 40:29

When you spiritually stretch beyond anything you have ever done before, then His power will flow into you. . . . The gospel of Jesus Christ is filled with His power, which is available to every earnestly seeking daughter or son of God. It is my testimony that when we draw His power into our lives, both He and we will rejoice.

ABIDING BY GOD'S LAWS

The law of the Lord is perfect, converting the soul:
the testimony of the Lord is sure, making wise the simple.
The statutes of the Lord are right, rejoicing the heart:
the commandment of the Lord is pure, enlightening the eyes.

PSALM 19:7–8

My dear brothers and sisters, divine laws are God's gifts to His children. Just as our family's rules kept our children safe as they grew to adulthood, just as divine laws governing the heart and the flight of airplanes keep you safe on an operating table or while traveling, abiding by God's laws will keep you safe as you progress toward eventual exaltation. Let me say it as succinctly as I can: As you abide by God's laws, you *are* progressing toward exaltation. . . . God's laws are motivated entirely by his infinite love for us and His desire for us to become all we can become.

HIS PATHWAY
TO PEACE

Now the Lord of peace himself give you peace always
by all means. The Lord be with you all.

2 THESSALONIANS 3:16

Prophecies of hope could materialize if leaders and citizens of nations would apply the teachings of Jesus Christ. Ours could then be an age of unparalleled peace and progress. Barbarism of the past would be buried. War with its horrors would be relegated to the realm of maudlin memory. Aims of nations would be mutually supportive. Peacemakers could lead in the art of arbitration, give relief to the needy, and bring hope to those who fear. Of such patriots, future generations would shout praises, and our Eternal God would pass judgments of glory.

The hope of the world is the Prince of Peace—our Creator, Savior, Jehovah, and Judge. He offers us the good life, the abundant life, and eternal life. Peaceful—even prosperous—living can come to those who abide His precepts and follow His pathway to peace. This I declare to all the world.

LEARN OF JESUS CHRIST

*Learn of me, and listen to my words; walk in the meekness
of my Spirit, and you shall have peace in me.*

DOCTRINE AND COVENANTS 19:23

If you proceed to learn *all* you can about Jesus Christ, I promise you that your love for Him, and for God's laws, will grow beyond what you currently imagine. I promise you also that your ability to turn away from sin will increase. Your desire to keep the commandments will soar. You will find yourself better able to walk away from the entertainment and entanglements of those who mock the followers of Jesus Christ.

THE DIVINE EXEMPLAR

For behold, he surely must die that salvation may come;
yea, it behooveth him and becometh expedient that he dieth,
to bring to pass the resurrection of the dead, that thereby
men may be brought into the presence of the Lord.

HELAMAN 14:15

God knew that because of the adversary's deceptive tactics and traps, the covenant path would not be easy to find or to stay on. So, He sent His Only Begotten Son to atone for us and to show us the way. The godly power available to all who love and follow Jesus Christ is the power to heal us, strengthen us, cleanse us from sin, and magnify us to do things we could never do on our own. Our Savior is the Divine Exemplar who marked the path that we are to follow.

PERCEPTIVE PREPARATION

*To every thing there is a season, and a time
to every purpose under the heaven:*

ECCLESIASTES 3:1

We who tarry here have a few precious moments
remaining "to prepare to meet God" (Alma 34:32).
Unfinished business is our worst business. Perpetual
procrastination must yield to perceptive preparation.
Today we have a little more time to bless others—time
to be kinder, more compassionate, quicker to thank and
slower to scold, more generous in sharing, more gracious
in caring.

OUR GREAT EXEMPLAR

He that saith he abideth in him ought himself
also so to walk, even as he walked.

1 JOHN 2:6

Jesus was our great exemplar. We can't ever achieve perfection in this life—that's not to be until the next world when our bodies will be changed—but we can follow His example.

You can read one evening about Jesus's responsibility as "Judge" and know that the day will come when each one of us will stand before Him to be judged. Then read of His responsibility as the "Millennial Messiah" and what that will mean when He will reign and rule from two world headquarters: from Jerusalem of old and from New Jerusalem in Jackson County. Then He will be King of kings and Lord of lords.

THE SECOND GREAT COMMANDMENT

Have we not all one father? hath not one God created us? why do we deal treacherously every man against his brother, by profaning the covenant of our fathers?

MALACHI 2:10

Regardless of where we call home, members of the Church feel passionately about the fatherhood of God and the brotherhood of man. Thus, *our* greatest joy comes as we help our brothers and sisters, no matter where we live in this wonderful world.

Giving help to others—making a conscientious effort to care about others as much as or *more* than we care about ourselves—is our joy. Especially, I might add, when it is not convenient and when it takes us out of our comfort zone. *Living* that second great commandment is the *key* to becoming a true disciple of Jesus Christ.

OUR SPIRITUAL WEALTH

But Jesus said, Suffer little children, and forbid them not,
to come unto me: for of such is the kingdom of heaven.

MATTHEW 19:14

Spiritual concerns are of great importance. Spiritually, we need children as much as they need us. They are our spiritual wealth. Children teach us the joy of building goodness that will outlive our own. They teach us the joy of loving someone more than self. That love lifts one to give from the abundance of one's own life to help a child. . . .

Future happiness and even the future of nations is linked to children. Families with children need to be re-enthroned as the fundamental unit of society. We simply must value children more than we do! Without a new generation to replace the old, there is no wealth; without families, there is no future.

JOY IN THE SABBATH

Speak thou also unto the children of Israel, saying,
Verily my sabbaths ye shall keep: for it is a sign between
me and you throughout your generations; that ye may
know that I am the Lord that doth sanctify you.

EXODUS 31:13

How can you ensure that your behavior on the Sabbath will lead to joy and rejoicing? In addition to your going to church, partaking of the sacrament, and being diligent in your specific call to serve, what other activities would help to make the Sabbath a delight for you? What sign will you give to the Lord to show your love for Him? . . .

Make the Sabbath a delight by rendering service to others, especially those who are not feeling well or those who are lonely or in need. Lifting their spirits will lift yours as well.

INDIVIDUAL JUDGMENT

But I say unto you, That every idle word that men shall speak,
they shall give account thereof in the day of judgment.
MATTHEW 12:36

An unchanging principle, brothers and sisters, is that of your eventual judgment. Each of you will be judged according to your individual works and the desires of your hearts. You will not be required to pay the debt of any other. Your eventual placement in the celestial, terrestrial, or telestial kingdom will not be determined by chance. The Lord has prescribed unchanging requirements for each. You can know what the scriptures teach, and pattern your lives accordingly.

ULTIMATE HOPE

For in thee, O Lord, do I hope:
thou wilt hear, O Lord my God.

PSALM 38:15

Happiness comes when scriptures are used in shaping our lives. They speak of the "brightness of hope" for which we yearn (2 Nephi 31:20). But if our hopes were narrowly confined only to moments in mortality, we should surely be disappointed. Our ultimate hope must be anchored to the Atonement of the Lord. . . .

An understanding of that objective should help us approach the future with faith instead of fear, with a more excellent hope in place of despair. God sent each of us here to be happy and successful.

TAKING UPON THE NAME OF JESUS CHRIST

I will declare thy name unto my brethren:
in the midst of the congregation will I praise thee.

PSALM 22:22

Every Sunday as we worthily partake of the sacrament, we make anew our sacred promise to our Heavenly Father that we are willing to take upon us the name of His Son, Jesus Christ. We promise to follow Him, repent, keep His commandments, and *always* remember Him.

When we omit His name from His Church, we are inadvertently removing *Him* as the central focus of our lives.

Taking the Savior's name upon us includes declaring and witnessing to others—through our actions and our words—that Jesus is the Christ.

TURN TO
THE SCRIPTURES

*Search the scriptures; for in them ye think ye have
eternal life: and they are they which testify of me.*

JOHN 5:39

Motivation for scriptural guidance comes when important choices must be made—even between options that are equally right. The Brethren are often faced with these kinds of decisions. On such an occasion, we turn to the scriptures. We may read all of the standard works afresh, looking for insights relative to a specific issue. . . .

We all *need* guidance through life. We *obtain* it best from the standard works and teachings of the prophets of God. With diligent effort, we can *achieve* that guidance and thus qualify for all of the blessings that God has in store for His faithful children.

TRUE PARTNERS

*Now I beseech you, brethren, by the name of our
Lord Jesus Christ, . . . that there be no divisions
among you; but that ye be perfectly joined together
in the same mind and in the same judgment.*

1 CORINTHIANS 1:10

There is great power in a strong partnership. True
partners can achieve more than the sum of each acting
alone. With true partners, one plus one is much more
than two. For example, Dr. Will Mayo and his brother,
Dr. Charles Mayo, formed the Mayo Clinic. Lawyers
and others form important partnerships. And in marriage, a husband and wife can form *the* most significant
partnership of all—an eternal family.

Sustainable improvements in any endeavor depend
on collaboration and agreement. Great leaders and partners develop the skill of sharing insights and efforts and
the pattern of building consensus. Great partners are
completely loyal. They suppress personal ego in exchange
for being part of creating something larger than themselves. Great partnerships depend upon each partner developing his or her own personal attributes of character.

PLACE OF GATHERING

For there shall be a day, that the watchmen upon
the mount Ephraim shall cry, Arise ye, and let
us go up to Zion unto the Lord our God.

JEREMIAH 31:6

The choice to come unto Christ is not a matter of physical location; it is a matter of individual commitment. All members of the Church have access to the doctrine, ordinances, priesthood keys, and blessings of the gospel, regardless of their location. . . .

True, in the early days of the Church, conversion often meant emigration as well. But now the gathering takes place in each nation. The Lord has decreed the establishment of Zion in each realm where He has given His Saints their birth and nationality. The place of gathering for Brazilian Saints is in Brazil; the place of gathering for Nigerian Saints is in Nigeria; the place of gathering for Korean Saints is in Korea. Zion is "the pure in heart" (Doctrine and Covenants 97:21). It is wherever righteous Saints are.

THE HEART
OF THE CHURCH

For by one Spirit are we all baptized into one body, whether we be Jews or Gentiles, whether we be bond or free; and have been all made to drink into one Spirit. For the body is not one member, but many.

1 CORINTHIANS 12:13–14

We need to keep the heart of the Church strong in order to keep pace with growth elsewhere. We need to rescue those among us who are not presently participating as actively as they might. We need their strength, and, more importantly, they need the blessings that will thereby come to them and their families.

LEADERSHIP AND LAW

Lead me in thy truth, and teach me: for thou art the God of my salvation; on thee do I wait all the day.

PSALM 25:5

Prophets of God have many attributes in common. One is that each prophet understands the importance of divine law. The knowledge of divine law and effective, righteous leadership go hand in hand. The more of God's laws you know—and more importantly, live—the more effective your righteous leadership will be. . . .

Divine law is incontrovertible and irrefutable. Divine law cannot be denied or disputed. And when God's laws are obeyed, relevant blessings *always* result! Blessings are always predicated upon obedience to applicable law.

THE GIFT OF DISCERNMENT

Wherefore, beware lest ye are deceived; and that ye may not be deceived seek ye earnestly the best gifts, always remembering for what they are given.

DOCTRINE AND COVENANTS 46:8

Prayer is a key. Pray to know what to stop doing and what to start doing. Pray to know what to add to your environment and what to remove so the Spirit can be with you in abundance.

Plead with the Lord for the gift of discernment. Then live and work to be worthy to receive that gift so that when confusing events arise in the world, you will know exactly what is true and what is not.

REPENTANCE AND RESTITUTION

Repent ye therefore, and be converted, that your sins may be blotted out, when the times of refreshing shall come from the presence of the Lord.

ACTS 3:19

In your journey through life, you meet many obstacles and make some mistakes. Scriptural guidance helps you to recognize error and make necessary correction. You stop going in the wrong direction. You carefully study the scriptural road map. Then you proceed with repentance and restitution required to get on the "strait and narrow path which leads to eternal life" (2 Nephi 31:18).

Brothers and sisters, our busy lives force us to focus on things we *do* from day to day. But the development of character comes only as we focus on who we really *are*. To establish and accomplish those greater goals, we do need heavenly help.

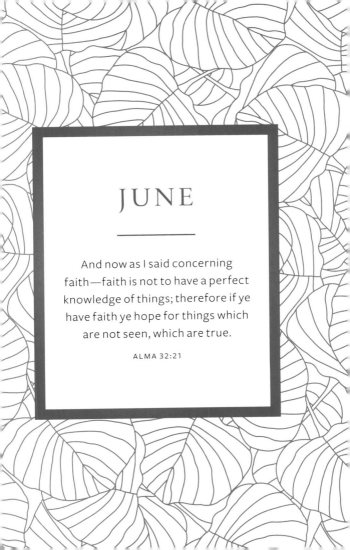

JUNE

And now as I said concerning faith—faith is not to have a perfect knowledge of things; therefore if ye have faith ye hope for things which are not seen, which are true.

ALMA 32:21

NOBLE AND GREAT

Now the Lord had shown unto me, Abraham, the intelligences that were organized before the world was; and among all these there were many of the noble and great ones.

ABRAHAM 3:22

You are one of God's noble and great spirits, held in reserve to come to earth at this time. In your premortal life you were appointed to help prepare the world for the great gathering of souls that will precede the Lord's Second Coming. You are one of a covenant people. You are an heir to the promise that all the earth will be blessed by the seed of Abraham and that God's covenant with Abraham will be fulfilled through his lineage in these latter days.

As a member of the Church, you have made sacred covenants with the Lord. You have taken upon yourself the name of Jesus Christ. You have promised to always remember Him and to keep His commandments. In return, He has agreed to grant His Spirit to be with you.

LEARN YOUR TALENTS

For all have not every gift given unto them; for there are many gifts, and to every man is given a gift by the Spirit of God.

DOCTRINE AND COVENANTS 46:11

Now and in the future, learn where your talents may be. Each one of us is unique, with special capabilities. We do not look alike and cannot be alike in the share of life's work we are to do. But as you lose yourself in service of worth to others, something wonderful will happen to you. Your life may stand as a monument to greatness, anchored to the pedestal of trust, crowned with the flower of achievement, and glistening with the brightness of your own joy.

THE WORD OF WISDOM

If any man defile the temple of God, him shall God destroy;
for the temple of God is holy, which temple ye are.

1 CORINTHIANS 3:17

A step toward self-mastery comes from obedience to the Word of Wisdom. . . . As you develop courage to say no to alcohol, tobacco, and other stimulants, you gain additional strength. You can then refuse conspiring men—those seditious solicitors of harmful substances or smut. You can reject their evil enticements to your body.

If you yield to anything that can addict, and thus defy the Word of Wisdom, your spirit surrenders to the body. The *flesh* then enslaves the *spirit*. This is contrary to the purpose of your mortal existence. And in the process of such addiction, your life span is likely to be shortened, thereby reducing the time available for repentance by which your spirit might attain self-mastery over your body.

LIGHT IN THE DARK

The people that walked in darkness have seen a great light: they that dwell in the land of the shadow of death, upon them hath the light shined.

ISAIAH 9:2

Because of the Savior's sacrifice, we have access to His healing power. He will heal our hearts, give us strength when we are weak, enable us to do things we could never do on our own and heal us from sin when we repent. . . .

Life can be overwhelming at times. My wife Dantzel died suddenly when her heart stopped beating. All my knowledge as a heart surgeon could not save her. Cancer has claimed the lives of two of our daughters. I understand the heartbreak of separation from loved ones.

But Jesus is the Light that shines in the dark.

LIVING PURE RELIGION

We believe that religion is instituted of God.

DOCTRINE AND COVENANTS 134:4

Some challenge the relevance of religion in modern life. As in every age, so today there are those who mock or decry the free exercise of religion. Some even blame religion for any number of the world's ills. Admittedly, there have been times when atrocities have been committed in the name of religion. But living the Lord's pure religion, which means striving to become a true disciple of Jesus Christ, is a way of life and a daily commitment that will provide divine guidance. As you practice your religion, you are exercising your faith. You are letting your faith show.

HUSBANDS AND FATHERS

*I, Nephi, having been born of goodly parents, therefore I
was taught somewhat in all the learning of my father.*

1 NEPHI 1:1

Husbands and fathers: With your dear partner, shape
attitudes at home. Establish a pattern of prayer. Pray regularly and vocally for your priesthood and auxiliary leaders, both local and general. Your manners of courtesy at
home and of reverence in the chapel will be copied by
members of your family. Help your loved ones follow
proper channels when they seek guidance. Teach that
counsel should be obtained from trusted parents and
leaders on a local level, not from General Authorities.

ROOTED TO JESUS CHRIST

*The Lord is my strength and song, and he is become
my salvation: he is my God, and I will prepare him an
habitation; my father's God, and I will exalt him.*

EXODUS 15:2

Consider the coconut tree. Its fruit gives us food when we are hungry. Its water gives us drink when we are thirsty. Its branches give us shade from the sun, shelter for our homes, and so much more. We praise the coconut tree for its great value.

But a tree cannot bear good fruit without good roots. While we may praise the fruits of the gospel, we must acknowledge the roots. Members of this Church are rooted to the rock of our salvation, who is Jesus Christ. He is the source of our strength. His is the love that nourishes us. He is the Son of the living God.

NOTHING OF GREATER CONSEQUENCE

He hath abounded toward us in all wisdom and
prudence; having made known unto us the mystery of
his will . . . : That in the dispensation of the fulness of
times he might gather together in one all things in Christ,
both which are in heaven, and which are on earth.

EPHESIANS 1:8–10

The gathering of Israel ultimately means offering the gospel of Jesus Christ to God's children on both sides of the veil who have neither made crucial covenants with God nor received their essential ordinances.

Every child of our Heavenly Father deserves the opportunity to *choose* to follow Jesus Christ, to accept and receive His gospel with all of its blessings—yes, all the blessings that God promised to the lineage of Abraham, Isaac, and Jacob, who, as you know, is also known as Israel.

My dear extraordinary youth, you were sent to earth at this precise time, the most crucial time in the history of the world, to help gather Israel. There is *nothing* happening on this earth right now that is more important than that. There is *nothing* of greater consequence. Absolutely *nothing*.

A RAFTING TRIP
THROUGH LIFE

The foundation of God standeth sure.

2 TIMOTHY 2:19

We are all, metaphorically speaking, on a rafting trip through life. Some of the trip is beautiful and peaceful, but at some point we all hit rapids. As we face the churning challenges of our lives, the greatest and only real safety comes as we hold on to the raft, which is the restored gospel of Jesus Christ. Clinging to others can help as we minister to each other, but *not* if it means letting go of the raft.

WORTHY SIGHTS
AND SOUNDS

And that which doth not edify is not of God, and is darkness.
That which is of God is light; and he that receiveth light,
and continueth in God, receiveth more light; and that light
groweth brighter and brighter until the perfect day.

DOCTRINE AND COVENANTS 50:23–24

Dear brothers and sisters, please fill your minds with worthy sights and sounds. Cultivate your precious gift of the Holy Ghost. Protect it as the priceless gift that it is. Carefully listen for its quiet communication. You will be spiritually stronger if you do. . . . As you control your thoughts, you control your actions. Indeed, worthy music can provide power and protection for your soul.

GOD'S PERFECT LOVE

Jesus knew that his hour was come that he should depart out of this world unto the Father, having loved his own which were in the world, he loved them unto the end.

JOHN 13:1

God loves every one of us with perfect love. More than anything, our Father wants His children to *choose* to return home to Him. Everything He does is motivated by His yearning desire. The entire reason we are on this earth is to qualify to live with Him forever. We do that by using our agency to find and stay on the covenant path that leads back to our heavenly home. . . .

Because the Father and the Son love us with infinite, perfect love, and because They know we cannot see everything They see, They have given us laws that will guide and protect us.

ONE WITH GOD

*That they all may be one; as thou, Father, art in me,
and I in thee, that they also may be one in us: that
the world may believe that thou hast sent me.*

JOHN 17:21

Let us now ponder the deep meaning of the word
atonement. In the English language, the components
are *at-one-ment*, suggesting that a person is at one with
another. Other languages employ words that connote
either *expiation* or *reconciliation*. *Expiation* means "to
atone for." *Reconciliation* . . . means "to sit again with."

Rich meaning is found in study of the word *atonement* in the Semitic languages of Old Testament times.
In Hebrew, the basic word for atonement is *kaphar*, a
verb that means "to cover over" or "to forgive." Closely
related is the Aramaic and Arabic word *kafat*, meaning
"a close embrace.". . .

I weep for joy when I contemplate the significance of
it all. To be redeemed is to be atoned—received in the
close embrace of God with an expression not only of His
forgiveness, but of our oneness of heart and mind.

THE GIFT OF
THE SABBATH

And they returned, and prepared spices and ointments; and
rested the sabbath day according to the commandment.

LUKE 23:56

I first found delight in the Sabbath many years ago when, as a busy surgeon, I knew that the Sabbath became a day for personal healing. By the end of each week, my hands were sore from repeatedly scrubbing them with soap, water, and a bristle brush. I also needed a breather from the burden of a demanding profession. Sunday provided much-needed relief.

What did the Savior mean when He said that "the Sabbath was made for man, and not man for the Sabbath" (Mark 2:27)? I believe He wanted us to understand the Sabbath was His gift to us, granting real respite from the rigors of daily life and an opportunity for spiritual and physical renewal. God gave us this special day, not for amusement or daily labor but for a rest from duty, with physical and spiritual relief.

OPENING THE HEAVENS

But if from thence thou shalt seek the Lord
thy God, thou shalt find him, if thou seek him
with all thy heart and with all thy soul.

DEUTERONOMY 4:29

Our Savior and Redeemer, Jesus Christ, will perform some of His mightiest works between now and when He comes again. We will see miraculous indications that God the Father and His Son, Jesus Christ, preside over this Church in majesty and glory. But in coming days, it will not be possible to survive spiritually without the guiding, directing, comforting, and constant influence of the Holy Ghost.

My beloved brothers and sisters, I plead with you to increase your spiritual capacity to receive revelation. . . . Choose to do the spiritual work required to enjoy the gift of the Holy Ghost and hear the voice of the Spirit more frequently and more clearly.

FACING UPWARDS

Nevertheless, I did look unto my God, and
I did praise him all the day long.

1 NEPHI 18:16

Trees reach up for the light and grow in the process. So do we as sons and daughters of heavenly parents. Facing upwards provides a loftier perspective than facing right or facing left. Looking up in search of holiness builds strength and dignity as disciples of Deity. . . .

In rendering service to others, which way do we face? From the right or the left, we can only push or pull. We can lift only from a higher plane. To reach it we don't look sideways; we look up to our Master. Just as we must look to God to live well, so we must look to God to serve well.

FAITH NOW, FAITH LATER

Wherefore, whoso believeth in God might with surety hope for a better world, yea, even a place at the right hand of God, which hope cometh of faith, maketh an anchor to the souls of men, which would make them sure and steadfast, always abounding in good works, being led to glorify God.

ETHER 12:4

All that the future holds in store for each sacred child of God will be shaped by his or her parents, family, friends, and teachers. Thus, our faith *now* becomes part of our posterity's faith *later*.

Each individual will make his or her way in a constantly changing world—a world of competing ideologies. The forces of evil will ever be in opposition to the forces of good. Satan constantly strives to influence us to follow his ways and make us miserable, even as he is. And the normal risks of life, such as illness, injury, and accident, will ever be present.

We live in a time of turmoil. . . . But we do not need to let our fears displace our faith. We can combat those fears by strengthening our faith.

TIME TO PREPARE

Jesus said unto her, I am the resurrection, and the
life: he that believeth in me, though he were dead,
yet shall he live: And whosoever liveth and believeth
in me shall never die. Believest thou this?

JOHN 11:25–26

Now is the time to prepare. Then, when death comes, we can move toward the celestial glory that Heavenly Father has prepared for His faithful children. Meanwhile, for sorrowing loved ones left behind . . . the sting of death is soothed by a steadfast faith in Jesus Christ, a perfect brightness of hope, a love of God and of all men, and a deep desire to serve them. That faith, that hope, that love will qualify us to come into God's holy presence and, with our eternal companions and families, dwell with Him forever.

GREAT SPIRITUAL STRENGTH

And his disciples asked him, saying, Master, who did sin,
this man, or his parents, that he was born blind?
Jesus answered, Neither hath this man sinned, nor his parents:
but that the works of God should be made manifest in him.

JOHN 9:2–3

For reasons usually unknown, some people are born with physical limitations. Specific parts of the body may be abnormal. Regulatory systems may be out of balance. And all of our bodies are subject to disease and death. Nevertheless, the gift of a physical body is priceless. Without it, we cannot attain a fulness of joy.

A perfect body is not required to achieve a divine destiny. In fact, some of the sweetest spirits are housed in frail frames. Great spiritual strength is often developed by those with physical challenges precisely because they are challenged. Such individuals are entitled to all the blessings that God has in store for His faithful and obedient children.

INTEGRITY
OF TRUTH

*The just man walketh in his integrity:
his children are blessed after him.*

PROVERBS 20:7

Danger lurks when we divide ourselves with expressions such as "my private life," "my professional life," or even "my best behavior." Living life in separate compartments can lead to internal conflict and exhausting tension. . . . Inner peace comes only as we maintain the integrity of truth in all aspects of our lives. When we covenant to follow the Lord and obey his commandments, we accept His standards in *every* thought, action, and deed.

OUR JUDGMENT
INTERVIEW

I say unto you, can ye look up to God at that day with a
pure heart and clean hands? I say unto you, can you look up,
having the image of God engraven upon your countenances?

ALMA 5:19

Brothers and sisters, be of good cheer. Take life one
step at a time and do the best you can each day. Life
passes so swiftly. We do not know how many years we
may have together here in mortality. . . .

When mortal life is over, each of us will return to
God, who gave us life. In a Judgment interview, I doubt
that He will ask a surgeon, "How many operations did
you perform?" or "Do you wish you had spent more time
at the hospital?" But I *know* He will ask if Sister Nelson
and I remained faithful to our covenants to take upon
ourselves the name of Jesus Christ and always remember
Him. No doubt He will carefully scrutinize my apostolic
ministry, but that vital subject will probably be subordi-
nated to His evaluation of my record as a husband and
father.

GREATER WORTH

And we had obtained the records which the Lord had commanded us, and searched them and found that they were desirable; yea, even of great worth unto us, insomuch that we could preserve the commandments of the Lord unto our children.

1 NEPHI 5:21

My brothers and sisters, how precious *is* the Book of Mormon to you? If you were offered diamonds or rubies *or* the Book of Mormon, which would you choose? Honestly, which *is* of greater worth to you? . . .

Something powerful happens when a child of God seeks to know more about Him and His Beloved Son. Nowhere are those truths taught more clearly and powerfully than in the Book of Mormon.

THE PRIESTHOOD POWER OF WOMEN

Therefore, in the ordinances thereof,
the power of godliness is manifest.

DOCTRINE AND COVENANTS 84:20

When you are set apart to serve in a calling under the direction of one who holds priesthood keys—such as your bishop or stake president—you are given priesthood authority to function in that calling. Similarly, in the holy temple you are authorized to perform and officiate in priesthood ordinances *every time* you attend. Your temple endowment prepares you to do so. . . .

As a righteous, endowed Latter-day Saint woman, you speak and teach with power and authority from God. Whether by exhortation or conversation, we need your voice teaching the doctrine of Christ. We need your input in family, ward, and stake councils. Your participation is essential and never ornamental!

POWER OF PRAYER

*I will therefore that men pray every where, lifting
up holy hands, without wrath and doubting.*

1 TIMOTHY 2:8

Pray alone in your closet—in the solitude of your own sanctuary. Pour out the longings of your soul. Then pray with and for your [spouse], your sons and daughters, your sister and brother, your mother and father and all in your family. Let the weight of your innocence be felt as you lovingly motivate others to good works. With your mind so attuned to the Lord and His power, your influence for good becomes immeasurably great. And in this world of sin and temptation, the power of prayer will protect you and be a shield for your loved ones.

SATAN'S PURPOSE

*Pray always, that you may come off conqueror; yea, that
you may conquer Satan, and that you may escape the
hands of the servants of Satan that do uphold his work.*

DOCTRINE AND COVENANTS 10:5

What is Satan's purpose? It is to make people miserable. He has no body, and he's envious of those who do. So, Satan tempts you and me nearly every day. He tempts us through our appetites. Our Creator gave us appetites in order to perpetuate the species. We have an appetite for food, we have an appetite for drink, and we have an appetite for love. Without those appetites being fulfilled, there would be no perpetuation of the species and no fulfillment of God's great plan of happiness for His children. So how does Satan tempt us? Through those very appetites. He tempts us to eat things we should not eat, to drink things we should not drink, and to love in ways we should not love. Therefore, we have to be very careful to control our appetites so that we can enjoy the blessings of Heavenly Father and choose to follow His way of life.

LOYALTY AND LOVE

What therefore God hath joined together,
let not man put asunder.

MARK 10:9

Your highest personal priority is your spouse—husband to wife and wife to husband. Your commitment to each other is eternal. Your families—children and grandchildren—are yours forever. Through appropriate means, keep as close to them as you can. Even though distances between you may be great, let them feel what you are feeling as you serve the Lord in His work.

Loyalty to the Lord and love for your family are not to be competitive! They are to be synergistic! The Lord said that "thy duty is unto the church forever, and this because of thy family" (Doctrine and Covenants 23:3). An eternal family is the end. The Church is the means to that end. We are building eternal families!

MORE IN MIND

For I know the thoughts that I think toward you, saith the Lord,
thoughts of peace, and not of evil, to give you an expected end.
JEREMIAH 29:11

God has sent you here to be successful and to have joy in your journey in mortality. He wants you to know that "with God nothing shall be impossible" (Luke 1:37). You are entitled through your worthiness to receive revelation to help you with your righteous endeavors. You may take upon you the name of the Lord. You may pray in His holy name. You can qualify to speak in the sacred name of God. It matters not that times of tribulation will come. Your prayerful access to help is just as real as it was when David battled his Goliath. . . .

The Lord has more in mind for you than you have in mind for yourself! You have been reserved and preserved for this time and place. You can do hard things. At the same time, as you love Him and keep His commandments, great rewards—even unimaginable achievements—may be yours.

POWER IN THE PRIESTHOOD

That the rights of the priesthood are inseparably connected with the powers of heaven, and that the powers of heaven cannot be controlled nor handled only upon the principles of righteousness.

DOCTRINE AND COVENANTS 121:36

How . . . can we increase our power in the priesthood? We need to pray from our hearts. Polite recitations of past and upcoming activities, punctuated with some requests for blessings, cannot constitute the kind of communing with God that brings enduring power. Are you willing to pray *to know how to pray* for more power? The Lord will teach you.

Are you willing to search the scriptures and feast on the words of Jesus Christ—to study *earnestly* in order to have more power? . . .

Are you willing to worship in the temple regularly? The Lord loves to do His own teaching in His holy house. . . . Imagine the increase in priesthood power that could be yours.

INDIVIDUAL WORTHINESS

As ye know how we exhorted and comforted and charged every
one of you, as a father doth his children, that ye would walk
worthy of God, who hath called you unto his kingdom and glory.

1 THESSALONIANS 2:11–12

Individual worthiness to enter the Lord's house requires much individual spiritual preparation. But with the Lord's help, nothing is impossible. . . . Individual worthiness requires a total conversion of mind and heart to be more like the Lord, to be an honest citizen, to be a better example, and to be a holier person.

I testify that such preparatory work brings innumerable blessings in this life and inconceivable blessings for the life to come, including the perpetuation of your family unit throughout all eternity "in a state of never-ending happiness" (Mosiah 2:41).

TRUTH AND MERCY

Blessed be God, even the Father of our Lord Jesus Christ,
the Father of mercies, and the God of all comfort.

2 CORINTHIANS 1:3

Just as oxen may be equally yoked together to accomplish what one could not do alone, so the power of truth is augmented if equally yoked with righteousness or with mercy or with the spirit of love.

This concept . . . applies to our companions and children at home, where truth can even foment bitterness at times. Unless we couple truth with love and kindness, our focus may narrow to the tube of toothpaste squeezed at the top, the dust and cobwebs of work yet undone, the evidence of fingerprints on glass, or the hand-tools misplaced.

Truth, like justice, can be harsh and unforgiving when not tempered by mercy.

But when truth is magnified by mercy or refined by righteousness, it can be converted from a force that can destroy to a force that can bless.

INSPIRED QUESTIONS

Ask, and it shall be given you; seek, and ye shall find; knock, and it shall be opened unto you:

MATTHEW 7:7

Every one of us has questions. Seeking to learn, understand, and recognize truth is a vital part of our mortal experience. Much of my life has been spent in research. You too will learn best by asking inspired questions.

At this very moment some of you are struggling to know what you should be doing with your life. Others of you may wonder if you have been forgiven of your sins. . . .

Some may question why the Church does some of the things it does. Perhaps many of you are not sure how to get answers to your prayers.

Our Heavenly Father and His Son stand ready to respond to your questions through the ministering of the Holy Ghost. But it is up to you to learn how to qualify for and receive those answers.

JULY

Verily I say unto you all: Arise and
shine forth, that thy light may
be a standard for the nations.

DOCTRINE AND COVENANTS 115:5

ANCHOR TO OUR SOULS

*Wherein God, willing more abundantly to shew unto the heirs
of promise the immutability of his counsel, confirmed it by an
oath: That by two immutable things, in which it was impossible
for God to lie, we might have a strong consolation, who have
fled for refuge to lay hold upon the hope set before us: which
hope we have as an anchor of the soul, both sure and steadfast.*

HEBREWS 6:17–19

What does it mean for you that that gospel of Jesus
Christ has been restored to the earth?

It means that you and your family can be sealed
together forever! It means that because you have been
baptized by one who has authority from Jesus Christ and
have been confirmed a member of His Church, you can
enjoy the constant companionship of the Holy Ghost.
He will guide and protect you. It means you will never
be left comfortless or without access to the power of God
to help you. It means that priesthood power can bless
you as you receive essential ordinances and make covenants with God and keep them. What an anchor to our
souls are these truths, especially during these times when
the tempest is raging.

ENDURING LOVE

*Husbands, love your wives, even as Christ also
loved the church, and gave himself for it.*

EPHESIANS 5:25

Enduring love provides enduring lift through life's trials. An enduring marriage results when both husband and wife regard their union as one of the two most important commitments they will ever make.

The other commitment of everlasting consequence is to the Lord. Unfortunately, some souls make a covenant with God—signified by the sacred ordinance of baptism—without a heartfelt commitment to endure with Him. Baptism is an extremely important ordinance. But it is only initiatory. The supreme benefits of membership in the Church can only be realized only through the exalting ordinances of the temple. . . .

Without a strong commitment to the Lord, an individual is more prone to have a low level of commitment to a spouse. Weak commitments to eternal covenants lead to losses of eternal consequence.

MEMBER-MISSIONARY WORK

Even before they were born, they, with many others,
received their first lessons in the world of spirits and were
prepared to come forth in the due time of the Lord to labor
in his vineyard for the salvation of the souls of men.

DOCTRINE AND COVENANTS 138:56

Could a loving Father in Heaven, who commanded us to preach the gospel to every creature, ever draw a line of distinction between those who had never heard the gospel and those who had once heard and then forgotten?

Surely the answer is no. The work of salvation excludes no one! Missionaries and members of The Church of Jesus Christ of Latter-day Saints are sent forth to labor in the Lord's vineyard for the salvation of the souls of men. This includes member-missionary work at its best, with activation of less-active members and preparation of God's children for the blessings of the temple. God wants all of His children to qualify for eternal life.

PEACE IS POSSIBLE

Depart from evil, and do good;
seek peace, and pursue it.

PSALM 34:14

Because of the long history of hostility upon the earth, many feel that peace is beyond hope. I disagree. Peace is possible. We can learn to love our fellow human beings throughout the world. Whether they be Jewish, Islamic, or fellow Christians, whether Hindu, Buddhist, or other, we can live together with mutual admiration and respect, without forsaking our religious convictions. Things we have in common are greater than our differences.

CONNECTED THROUGH PRAYER

Then shall ye call upon me, and ye shall go and pray unto me, and I will hearken unto you. And ye shall seek me, and find me, when ye shall search for me with all your heart.

JEREMIAH 29:12–13

Please help your children to know how to pray to Heavenly Father. Jesus taught us how to pray. We pray to God, our Eternal Father, in the name of Jesus Christ, through the power of the Holy Ghost. That connection will give them strength. Never let them feel that they are alone.

DOUBT NOT, FEAR NOT

Look unto me in every thought;
doubt not, fear not.

DOCTRINE AND COVENANTS 6:36

True disciples of Jesus Christ are willing to stand out, speak up, and be different from the people of the world. They are undaunted, devoted, and courageous. . . . There is nothing easy or automatic about becoming such powerful disciples. Our focus must be riveted on the Savior and His gospel. It is mentally rigorous to strive to look unto Him in *every* thought. But when we do, our doubts and fears flee. . . . Faith in Jesus Christ propels us to do things we otherwise would not do. Faith that motivates us to action gives us more access to His power.

JOY, NOT GUILT TRIPS

There hath no temptation taken you but such as is common to man: but God is faithful, who will not suffer you to be tempted above that ye are able; but will with the temptation also make a way to escape, that ye may be able to bear it.

1 CORINTHIANS 10:13

Each of us is far from perfect, both spiritually and temporally. Reminders come repeatedly. We may lock keys inside the car, or even forget where the car is parked. And not infrequently we walk intently from one part of the house to another, only to forget the reason for the errand.

When comparing one's personal performance with the supreme standard of the Lord's expectation, the reality of imperfection can at times be depressing. My heart goes out to conscientious Saints who, because of their shortcomings, allow feelings of depression to rob them of happiness in life.

We all need to remember: men are that they might have joy—not guilt trips! We also need to remember that the Lord gives no commandments that are impossible to obey. But sometimes we fail to comprehend them fully.

JUDGMENTS AND CORRECTIONS

Behold, he who has repented of his sins, the same is forgiven, and I, the Lord, remember them no more.

DOCTRINE AND COVENANTS 58:42

Don't be depressed or discouraged because you aren't errorless. You do make mistakes, and if they are serious mistakes, you repent. Well, even if they are little mistakes, you repent. That is why you have an eraser; that is why you have a delete key on your keyboard. Those things are part of life. You make judgments, and you make corrections as you go.

LOYALTY TO THE LORD

*Surely the Lord God will do nothing, but he revealeth
his secret unto his servants the prophets.*

AMOS 3:7

Loyalty to the Lord carries an obligation of loyalty to
those called by the Lord to lead His Church. He has
empowered that men be ordained to speak in His holy
name. As they guide His unsinkable boat safely toward
the shore of salvation, we would do well to stay on board
with them. . . .

Nevertheless, some individuals want to jump "out of
the boat" before reaching land. And others, sadly, are
persuaded out by companions who insist that they know
more about life's perilous journey than do prophets of
the Lord. Problems often arise that are not of your own
making. Some of you may innocently find yourselves
abandoned by one you trusted. But you will never be
forsaken by your Redeemer.

IN HIS TIME

*For a small moment have I forsaken thee;
but with great mercies will I gather thee.*

ISAIAH 54:7

Bad things happen to good people. Accidents occur. Some married couples may not be blessed with children. Others may not marry in this life, or they may find themselves married to one who fails to keep the commandments. The Lord is aware of these circumstances. He will bestow all the blessings that He has in store for His faithful children—in His own way and in His own time. Be righteous, be patient, keep an eternal perspective, and you will be protected.

CORRECT PRINCIPLES

But he that doeth truth cometh to the light, that his deeds
may be made manifest, that they are wrought in God.

JOHN 3:21

The dismal dusk of today's spiritual drift provides a rare opportunity for the radiance of religion to light the way to a new tomorrow. This can happen only as we proclaim eternal truths that have the power to engender spiritual strength. Human nature cannot be changed by reforming public policy; that kind of change comes by exposing the human mind and heart to the transforming teachings of the Lord Jesus Christ. I have learned that when we teach His correct principles, people govern themselves appropriately.

SINS OF OMISSION

For he is the same yesterday, today, and forever; and the
way is prepared for all men from the foundation of the
world, if it so be that they repent and come unto him.

1 NEPHI 10:18

While the Lord insists on our repentance, most people don't feel such a compelling need. They include themselves among those who try to be good. They have no evil intent. Yet the Lord is clear in His message that *all* need to repent—not only from sins of *commission* but from sins of *omission* as well.

HEARTS IN HARMONY

And the Lord called his people Zion, because they
were of one heart and one mind, and dwelt in
righteousness; and there was no poor among them.

MOSES 7:18

A large church is something like a large person. Each requires a strong heart. Each one of you is an important part of the heart of the Church. I love a good, strong heart! I know that a heart works better if each part works in perfect harmony with the others. I also know that, if those fibers don't work in unison, the heart can stop pumping. This is just one of many lessons we can learn from the workings of the human heart.

As the Church continues to grow, it will bless the lives of more and more people throughout the world. So a larger heart and greater resources will be needed. From where do those resources come? They come from you, the faithful, tithe-paying members here at the heart of the Church. You dear members bear much of the burden of its growth.

THE LORD'S REWARDS

And it is requisite with the justice of God that men should be judged according to their works; and if their works were good in this life, and the desires of their hearts were good, that they should also, at the last day, be restored unto that which is good.

ALMA 41:3

Members of this Church invite all people to learn [eternal truths] and to qualify for eternal life. We invite all to gain faith in God the Eternal Father and in His Son, Jesus Christ, to repent, to receive the Holy Ghost, to obtain the blessings of the temple, to make and keep sacred covenants, and to endure to the end.

Mercifully, God's great plan of happiness and its eternal blessings can be extended to those who did not have the opportunity to hear the gospel in mortality. Temple ordinances can be done vicariously for them. . . .

Be we all reminded that, in the Lord's own way and time, no blessings will be withheld from His faithful Saints. The Lord will judge and reward each individual according to heartfelt desire as well as deed.

DESIRES OF OUR HEARTS

Every man may act in doctrine and principle . . . according to the moral agency which I have given unto him, that every man may be accountable for his own sins in the day of judgment.

DOCTRINE AND COVENANTS 101:78

Eventually you (and I) are going to die, be resurrected, be judged, and be awarded a place in eternal realms. With each passing sunset, you are closer to that inevitable day of judgment. Then you will be asked to account for your faith, your hopes, and your works. . . .

That judgment will consider not only your actions, but also your innermost intent and heartfelt desires. . . . The Lord knows the desires of our hearts. At the time of judgment, surely the special yearnings of single sisters and childless couples, for example, will be given compassionate consideration by Him. . . . He will know of your longings as [one] who tried diligently to serve your family and society properly.

TEACH YOUR CHILDREN

*And thou shalt teach them diligently unto thy
children, and shalt talk of them when thou sittest in
thine house, and when thou walkest by the way, and
when thou liest down, and when thou risest up.*

DEUTERONOMY 6:7

Read the scriptures to your children. Let them have
a turn reading. Some of the little ones will only be able
to hear your stories about Bible and Book of Mormon
characters, but they will be ready to read the scriptures
before you think they are ready. I think you can teach
your children how to read by reading from the Book of
Mormon. They will be the smartest children in school
because they will have learned how to read some very
difficult words. . . .

I would like for every child to memorize the sound of
his mother's voice, the sound of his father's voice, reading scriptures to them.

FOUNDATION OF THE CHURCH

Blessed be the God and Father of our Lord Jesus Christ,
who hath blessed us with all spiritual blessings in
heavenly places in Christ: according as he hath chosen
us in him before the foundation of the world, that we
should be holy and without blame before him in love.

EPHESIANS 1:3–4

This Church stands on a unique foundation, anchored to a bedrock of timeless truth. Brothers and sisters, the holy cause in which we are engaged did not begin in 1820 in the state of New York. It did not begin in Bethlehem. It did not begin in the Garden of Eden. The underpinnings of the everlasting gospel were in place even before the world was.

This reality is affirmed repeatedly in holy writ. I have studied the scriptures pertaining to that part of eternity before the earth was formed. . . . These unseen and timeless truths constitute "premortal pillars" that undergird the foundation of this Church.

LEARN TO LISTEN

Hearken, O ye people of my church, saith the voice of him who dwells on high, and whose eyes are upon all men; yea, verily I say: Hearken ye people from afar; and ye that are upon the islands of the sea, listen together.

DOCTRINE AND COVENANTS 1:1

Above all, God's children should learn to listen, then listen to learn from the Lord. On several sacred occasions in the world's history, our Heavenly Father has personally appeared to introduce His divine Son with a specific charge to "*hear* him" (Matthew 17:5; italics added). . . .

Your soul will be blessed as you learn to listen, then listen to learn from children, parents, partners, neighbors, and Church leaders, all of which will heighten capacity to hear counsel from on high.

Carefully listen to learn from the Lord through the still small voice—the Holy Spirit—which leads to truth. Listen to learn by studying scriptures that record His holy mind and will. Listen to learn in prayer, for He will answer the humble who truly seek Him.

INTENT TO OBEY

For he that receiveth my servants receiveth me.

DOCTRINE AND COVENANTS 84:36

Prophets see ahead. They see the harrowing dangers the adversary has placed or will yet place in our path. Prophets also foresee the grand possibilities and privileges awaiting those who listen *with the intent to obey*. I know this is true! I have experienced it for myself over and over again. . . .

You may not always understand every declaration of a living prophet. But when you know a prophet is a prophet, you can approach the Lord in humility and faith and ask for your witness about whatever His prophet has proclaimed.

PRINCIPLES THAT GOVERN HAPPINESS

He that keepeth the law, happy is he.
PROVERBS 29:18

Eternal principles that govern happiness apply equally to all. I doubt that the Lord cares much which honorable vocation you choose. But He does care if you love one another and serve one another. And He cares that you have the obedience and self-discipline needed to maintain your identity and honor your highest priorities.

SERVE YOUR NEIGHBOR

Behold, ye have called me your king; and if I,
whom ye call your king, do labor to serve you, then
ought not ye to labor to serve one another?

MOSIAH 2:18

We mingle on planet earth with neighbors—millions of them. To serve them, to satisfy them, and to lift them are exciting challenges. Interestingly, as we strive so to do, each servant becomes greater in the process. . . .

Satisfaction comes from service to others rendered well. It is love made visible. Conscientiously you may ask yourself: "When is it proper that I render a needed service, and when is it preferable to refer that individual to another?" As a surgeon, I was faced with this question on a daily basis. I accepted the responsibility for patient care only when I knew that I could render needed service as well as or better than anyone else available.

TONGUE OF
THE TOLERANT

*Ye will not suffer your children . . . that they transgress the laws
of God, and fight and quarrel one with another. . . . But ye
will teach them to walk in the ways of truth and soberness; ye
will teach them to love one another, and to serve one another.*

MOSIAH 4:14–15

God's children can be so intolerant with one another.
Neighboring factions . . . often develop animosity. Such
tendencies make me wonder: Cannot boundary lines
exist without becoming battle lines? Could not people
unite in waging war against the evils that beset mankind
instead of waging war on each other? Sadly, answers to
these questions are often no. Through the years, discrim-
ination based on ethnic or religious identity has led to
senseless slaughter, vicious pogroms, and countless acts
of cruelty. . . .

How different our world would be if all parents
would apply this inspired instruction [in Mosiah 4:14–
15]. . . . Men and women would respect their neighbors
and the beliefs held sacred by them. No longer would
ethnic jokes and cultural slurs be acceptable. The tongue
of the tolerant speaks no guile.

MIND AND HEART

*Yea, behold, I will tell you in your mind and in
your heart, by the Holy Ghost, which shall come
upon you and which shall dwell in your heart.*

DOCTRINE AND COVENANTS 8:2

As you ponder and pray about doctrinal principles, the
Holy Ghost will speak to your mind and your heart.
From events portrayed in the scriptures, new insights
will come and principles relevant to your situation will
distill upon your heart.

You cultivate such revelatory experiences by living
according to the light already given you and by searching the scriptures with pure motives—with real intent
to "come unto Christ" (Jacob 1:7). As you do so, your
confidence will "wax strong in the presence of God,"
and the Holy Ghost will be your constant companion
(Doctrine and Covenants 121:45).

STAND UPON OUR OWN FEET

Every man shall receive his own reward
according to his own labour.

1 CORINTHIANS 3:8

The monumental deeds of the pioneers descend as a weighty trust upon our shoulders. Those deeds are theirs, not ours. Their works cannot redound to our glory, but to our responsibility. We may claim no honor, no reward, no respect, nor special position, recognition, or credit because of what our forefathers were or what they wrought. We stand upon our own feet in our own shoes. We must develop our own understanding, rise by our own labor, and lift our own voices in living testimony.

WORTH THE PRICE

I say unto you, that likewise joy shall be in heaven
over one sinner that repenteth, more than over ninety
and nine just persons, which need no repentance.

LUKE 15:7

To repent from sin is not easy. But the prize is worth the price. Repentance needs to be done one step at a time. Humble prayer will facilitate each essential step. As prerequisites to forgiveness, there must first be recognition, remorse, then confession. . . .

Confession is to be made to the person who has been wronged. Confession should be sincere and not merely an admission of guilt after proof is evident. If many persons have been offended, confession should be made to all offended parties. Acts that may affect one's standing in the Church or the right to its privileges should be confessed promptly to the bishop. . . .

The next step is restitution—to repair damage done—if possible. Then come steps to resolve to do better and refrain from relapse—to repent "with full purpose of heart" (2 Nephi 31:13).

SACRED WORK

But I have prayed for thee, that thy faith fail not:
and when thou art converted, strengthen thy brethren.

LUKE 22:32

Of course, we are keenly interested in conversions, baptisms, and strengthening members of the Church. But if you have only one convert during your mission, I hope it would be yourself. Teaching the gospel is sacred work. There is not a better way to get the gospel of Jesus Christ into your heart and mind than for you to be a missionary and teach to others the resplendent and glorious gospel of the Lord Jesus Christ.

THE PRICE FOR PRIESTHOOD POWER

When thou saidst, Seek ye my face; my heart said
unto thee, Thy face, Lord, will I seek.

PSALM 27:8

In a coming day, *only* those men who have taken their priesthood seriously, by *diligently* seeking to be taught by the Lord Himself, will be able to bless, guide, protect, strengthen, and heal others. Only a man who has paid the price for priesthood power will be able to bring miracles to those he loves and keep his marriage and family safe, now and throughout eternity.

What is the price to develop such priesthood power? The Savior's senior Apostle, Peter, . . . declared qualities we should seek. . . . He named faith, virtue, knowledge, temperance, patience, godliness, brotherly kindness, charity, and diligence (see 2 Peter 1:5–10). And don't forget humility! So I ask, how would our family members, friends, and coworkers say you and I are doing in developing these and other spiritual gifts? The more those attributes are developed, the greater will be our priesthood power.

SURE IDENTITY
AND PRIORITY

*For in [the Lord] we live, and move, and have
our being; as certain also of your own poets
have said, For we are also his offspring.*

ACTS 17:28

My message . . . is about identity, priority, and blessings. An understanding of their interrelationship can help you deal better with life's challenges. It is important for you to know who you are and who you may become. It is more important than what you do, even as vital as your work is and will be. You pursue an education to prepare for life's work. But I want you also to prepare for life—eternal life. I emphasize this because some people on life's journey forget who they really are and what is really important. Without sure identity and priority, blessings that matter most are at the mercy of things that matter least.

LET YOUR FAITH SHOW

For ye are all the children of God by faith in Christ Jesus.

GALATIANS 3:26

When we speak of faith—the faith that can move mountains—we are not speaking of faith in general but of faith in the Lord Jesus Christ. Faith in the Lord Jesus Christ can be bolstered as we learn about Him and live our religion. The doctrine of Jesus Christ was designed by the Lord to help us increase our faith. . . . We might each ask ourselves, where is our faith? Is it in a team? Is it in a brand? Is it in a celebrity? Even the best teams can fail. Celebrities can fade. There is only One in whom your faith is always safe, and that is in the Lord Jesus Christ. And you need to let your faith show!

OUR ADVOCATE WITH THE FATHER

Wherefore he is able also to save them to the uttermost that come unto God by him, seeing he ever liveth to make intercession for them.

HEBREWS 7:25

Jesus is our Advocate with the Father. The word *advocate* comes from Latin roots meaning a "voice for" or "one who pleads for another." Other related terms are used in scripture, such as *mediator*. From the Book of Mormon we learn that this responsibility to mediate, or make intercession, was foreseen before His birth: Jesus "shall make intercession for all the children of men; and they that believe in him shall be saved" (2 Nephi 2:9).

This mission was clearly evident in the compassionate intercessory prayer of Jesus. In your mind, picture Him kneeling in fervent supplication. Listen to the beautiful language of His prayer. Sense His feeling for His weighty responsibility as mediator. . . .

Comprehending Him as our Advocate, Intercessor, and Mediator with the Father gives us assurance of His unequaled understanding, justice, and mercy.

YOUR OWN WITNESS

But, behold, I say unto you, that you must study it out
in your mind; then you must ask me if it be right, and
if it is right I will cause that your bosom shall burn
within you; therefore, you shall feel that it is right.

DOCTRINE AND COVENANTS 9:8

Does God really *want* to speak to you? Yes! . . . You don't have to wonder about what is true. You do not have to wonder whom you can safely trust. Through personal revelation, you can receive your own witness that the Book of Mormon is the word of God, that Joseph Smith is a prophet, and that this is the Lord's Church. Regardless of what others may say or do, no one can ever take away a witness borne to your heart and mind about what is true.

AUGUST

The Spirit itself beareth witness with
our spirit, that we are the children of
God: And if children, then heirs; heirs
of God, and joint-heirs with Christ; if so
be that we suffer with him, that we may
be also glorified together. For I reckon
that the sufferings of this present time
are not worthy to be compared with
the glory which shall be revealed in us.

ROMANS 8:16–18

THE LAW OF THE FAST

I would that ye should come unto Christ, who is the Holy One
of Israel, and partake of his salvation, and the power of his
redemption. Yea, come unto him, and offer your whole souls
as an offering unto him, and continue in fasting and praying,
and endure to the end; and as the Lord liveth ye will be saved.

OMNI 1:26

Let us not just talk of Christ or preach of Christ or employ a symbol representing Christ. Let us put our faith in the Lord Jesus Christ into action!

As you know, members of the Church observe the law of the fast one day each month. The doctrine of fasting is ancient. It has been practiced by biblical heroes from the earliest days. . . .

I *know* that God "has all power, all wisdom, and all understanding; he comprehendeth all things, and he is a merciful Being, even unto salvation, to those who will repent and believe on his name" (Alma 26:35). So, during times of deep distress . . . , the most natural thing for us to do is to call upon our Heavenly Father and His Son—the Master Healer—to show forth Their marvelous power to bless the people of the earth.

THE DIVINE COMMANDMENT OF TITHING

Will a man rob God? Yet ye have robbed me. But ye say,
Wherein have we robbed thee? In tithes and offerings.

MALACHI 3:8

We must be certain our own consciences are free from guilt. We must not rob or steal or shoplift or "anything like unto it" (Doctrine and Covenants 59:6). We can be protected from the disease of greed, which seems to underlie these problems, through the divine commandment of tithing. It gives great security. If a person learns to be honest in financial dealings with God, that individual is likely to be honest elsewhere, and success in life will ensue. . . . The law of tithing is a valuable key to the blessings of honesty and prosperity.

DISENGAGE FROM SOCIAL MEDIA

And this I speak for your own profit; not that I may cast a snare upon you, but for that which is comely, and that ye may attend upon the Lord without distraction.

1 CORINTHIANS 7:35

Disengage from a constant reliance on social media. . . . I acknowledge that there are positives about social media. But if you are paying more attention to feeds from social media than you are to the whisperings of the Spirit, then you are putting yourself at spiritual risk—as well as the risk of experiencing intense loneliness and depression. You and I both know youth who have been influenced through social media to do and say things that they never would do or say in person. Bullying is one example.

Another downside of social media is that it creates a false reality. Everyone posts their most fun, adventurous, and exciting pictures, which create the erroneous impression that everyone except you is leading a fun, adventurous, and exciting life. Much of what appears in your various social media feeds is distorted, if not fake.

FIRM FOUNDATIONS

It is upon the rock of our Redeemer, who is Christ, the Son of God, that ye must build your foundation; that when the devil shall send forth his mighty winds, . . . it shall have no power over you to drag you down to the gulf of misery and endless wo, because of the rock upon which ye are built, which is a sure foundation, a foundation whereon if men build they cannot fall.

HELAMAN 5:12

Just as buildings and institutions have foundations, so do we as individuals have foundations that support our faith. Some are weak; some are strong. We can waffle . . . , or we can stand on a firm foundation and anchor ourselves with straps of spiritual steel, rooted and grounded to the timeless pillars of the gospel. . . .

Even firm foundations cannot prevent life's problems. Wayward children cause parents to grieve. Some broken families don't get fixed. Gender disorientation is poorly understood. Married couples, for whatever reason, may not be blessed with children. Even in our day, "the guilty and the wicked go unpunished because of their money" (Helaman 7:5). Some things just don't seem fair.

With strong underpinnings, however, we are better able to reach upward for help, even when faced with questions without easy answers.

YOUR SPIRITUAL ATTRIBUTES

And again I would exhort you that ye would come unto Christ, and lay hold upon every good gift, and touch not the evil gift, nor the unclean thing.

MORONI 10:30

Your Heavenly Father has known you for a very long time. You, as His son or daughter, were chosen by Him to come to earth at this precise time, to be a leader in His great work on earth. You were chosen *not* for your bodily characteristics but for your *spiritual* attributes, such as bravery, courage, integrity of heart, a thirst for truth, a hunger for wisdom, and a desire to serve others.

You developed some of these attributes premortally. Others you can develop here on earth as you persistently seek them.

PRIMARY PURPOSE OF THE BOOK OF MORMON

Thus we may see that the Lord is merciful unto all who will, in the sincerity of their hearts, call upon his holy name. Yea, thus we see that the gate of heaven is open unto all, even to those who will believe on the name of Jesus Christ, who is the Son of God.

HELAMAN 3:27–28

Study of the Book of Mormon is most rewarding when one focuses on its *primary* purpose—to testify of Jesus Christ. By comparison, all other issues are incidental.

When you read the Book of Mormon, concentrate on the principal figure in the book—from its first chapter to the last—the Lord Jesus Christ, Son of the Living God. And look for a second undergirding theme: God will keep His covenants with the remnants of the house of Israel.

The Book of Mormon is a crucial component of that covenant.

ETERNAL SIGNIFICANCE

For I am about to restore many things to the earth, pertaining to the priesthood, saith the Lord of Hosts.

DOCTRINE AND COVENANTS 127:8

Because of the Lord Jesus Christ, the priesthood, the scriptures, and words of living prophets have eternal significance. Restoration of priesthood authority is important because it is the *power* of the Lord. Scriptures are important because they contain the *will* of the Lord. Prophets and apostles are important because they *teach and testify* of the Lord.

EASE THE BURDEN OF OTHERS

Surely he hath borne our griefs, and carried our sorrows:
yet we did esteem him stricken, smitten of God, and
afflicted. But he was wounded for our transgressions, he
was bruised for our iniquities: the chastisement of our
peace was upon him; and with his stripes we are healed.

ISAIAH 53:4–5

Yes, your Redeemer knows exactly how you feel. He knows your heart. And in time, He may inspire you to rise from your state of unbearable grief and reach out to ease the burden of some other suffering soul. Jesus taught that, "He that loseth his life for my sake shall find it" (Matthew 10:39). When you serve others, do so out of love for them and for your Savior. And He will heal you.

WITNESSES OF JESUS CHRIST

And said unto the woman, Now we believe, not because of thy saying: for we have heard him ourselves, and know that this is indeed the Christ, the Saviour of the world.

JOHN 4:42

The Bible and the Book of Mormon are both witnesses of Jesus Christ. They teach that He is the Son of God, that He lived an exemplary life, that He atoned for all mankind, that He died upon the cross and rose again as the resurrected Lord. They teach that He is the Savior of the world.

Scriptural witnesses authenticate each other. Each book refers to the other. Each book stands as evidence that God lives and speaks to his children by revelation to his prophets. Love for the Book of Mormon expands one's love for the Bible, and vice versa.

A DUAL BEING

The spirit and the body are the soul of man.
DOCTRINE AND COVENANTS 88:15

Each one of us . . . is a dual being—a biological (physical) entity, and an intellectual (spiritual) entity. The combination of both is intimate throughout mortality.

In the beginning, man, as that intellectual entity, was with God. Our intelligence was not created or made, nor can it be. That spirit, joined with a physical body of such remarkable qualities, becomes a living soul of supernal worth. . . .

Why were we created? Why are we here? Why are we upon the earth?

God has made it plain over and over again that the world was made for mankind to exist. We are here to work out our divine destiny, according to an eternal plan presented to us in the great council of heaven. Our bodies have been created to accommodate our spirits, to allow us to experience the challenges of mortality.

EQUAL
POTENTIAL

That you may be equal in the bonds of heavenly things, yea, and earthly things also, for the obtaining of heavenly things.

DOCTRINE AND COVENANTS 78:5

Blessings of the priesthood are shared by men and women. All may qualify for baptism and the gift of the Holy Ghost. All may take upon themselves the name of the Lord and partake of the sacrament. All may pray and receive answers to their prayers. Gifts of the Spirit and testimonies of the truth are bestowed regardless of gender. Men and women receive the highest ordinance in the house of the Lord together and equally, or not at all.

Opportunities for development of spiritual and intellectual potential are equal. Masculinity has no monopoly on the mind, and femininity has no exclusive dominion over the heart. The highest titles of human achievement—teacher, educated professional, loyal employee, faithful friend, student of the scriptures, child of God, disciple of Christ, trusted companion, loving parent—are earned under a uniform requirement of worthiness.

POWER OF GOD'S LOVE

Behold, my bowels are filled with compassion towards you. Have ye any that are sick among you? . . . Have ye any that are lame, or blind, or halt, or maimed, or leprous, or that are withered, or that are deaf, or that are afflicted in any manner? Bring them hither and I will heal them, for I have compassion upon you; my bowels are filled with mercy.

3 NEPHI 17:6–7

The Book of Mormon describes *how* one is born of God and *how* one gains the power to love as He does. It identifies three core principles that bring the power of God's love into our lives.

First, the Book of Mormon teaches that exercising faith in Christ and entering into a *covenant* with Him to keep His commandments is the key to being reborn spiritually. . . .

Second, the Savior Himself teaches that the power to become more like Him comes through receiving the *ordinances* of the gospel. . . .

Third, He exhorts us to *follow His example:* "What manner of men ought ye to be?" He asks rhetorically. His answer: "Verily I say unto you, even as I am" (3 Nephi 27:27). Truly, He wants us to become more like Him.

THE PRINCIPLE OF REVELATION

If any of you lack wisdom, let him ask of God, that giveth to all men liberally, and upbraideth not; and it shall be given him.

JAMES 1:5

What wisdom do you lack? What do you feel an urgent need to know or understand? Follow the example of the Prophet Joseph. Find a quiet place where you can regularly go. Humble yourself before God. Pour out your heart to your Heavenly Father. Turn to Him for answers and for comfort.

Pray in the name of Jesus Christ about your concerns, your fears, your weaknesses—yes, the very longings of your heart. And then listen! Write the thoughts that come to your mind. Record your feelings and follow through with actions that you are prompted to take. As you repeat this process day after day, month after month, year after year, you will "grow into the principle of revelation" (*Teachings of Presidents of the Church: Joseph Smith* [2007], 132).

JOY TO THE WORLD

Behold, God is my salvation; I will trust, and not be afraid: for the Lord Jehovah is my strength and my song; he also is become my salvation. Therefore with joy shall ye draw water out of the wells of salvation.

ISAIAH 12:2–3

When the focus of our lives is on God's plan of salvation, . . . and Jesus Christ and His gospel, we can feel joy regardless of what is happening—or not happening—in our lives. Joy comes from and because of Him. He is the source of all joy. We feel it at Christmastime when we sing, "Joy to the world, the Lord is come." And we can feel it all year round. For Latter-day Saints, Jesus Christ is joy!

That is why our missionaries leave their homes to preach His gospel. Their goal is not to increase the number of Church members. Rather, our missionaries teach and baptize to bring joy to the people of the world!

GATHERING ISRAEL

I have prepared thee for a greater work. Thou shalt
preach the fulness of my gospel, which I have sent forth
in these last days, the covenant which I have sent forth
to recover my people, which are of the house of Israel.

DOCTRINE AND COVENANTS 39:11

Would you like to help gather Israel during these precious latter days? Would you, who are the elect, be willing to help find the elect who have not heard the message of the restored gospel? . . .

Now, participating in the gathering of Israel will require some sacrifice on your part. It may even require some changes in your life. It will definitely take some of your time and energy and your God-given talents. Are you interested?

Just think of the excitement and urgency of it all: every prophet commencing with Adam has seen our day. And every prophet has talked about *our* day, when Israel would be gathered and the world would be prepared for the Second Coming of the Savior. Think of it! Of all the people who have ever lived on planet earth, we are the ones who get to participate in this final, great gathering event.

SPIRITUAL FREEDOM

Stand fast therefore in the liberty wherewith Christ hath made us free, and be not entangled again with the yoke of bondage.

GALATIANS 5:1

Freedom is more than material. It is more than political. It is a mental, spiritual force. Freedom reaches full fruition when it achieves spiritual fulfillment. Once I read of a prisoner of war, deprived of all material, political, and physical freedoms, who gained power to survive the ordeal as he forged from his memory verses from the Bible, which he wrote on scraps of bathroom tissue with stubs of lead pencil. While yet in physical bondage, he conceived his own spiritual liberty. He terminated restless torment by self-surrender to a greater power.

THE MAJESTY OF CREATION

But now, O Lord, thou art our father; we are the clay, and
thou our potter; and we all are the work of thy hand.

ISAIAH 64:8

The process of construction is truly inspiring to me. From conception to completion, any major building project reflects upon the work of the Master Creator. In fact, the Creation—of planet earth and of life upon it—undergirds all other creative capability. Any manmade creation is possible only because of our divine Creator. The people who design and build are given life and capacity by that Creator. And all materials used in the construction of an edifice are ultimately derived from the rich resources of the earth. . . .

It is difficult for mortal minds to comprehend the majesty of the Creation. . . . But I would like to stretch our minds to think of things beyond our easy grasp. The creation of man and woman was wondrous and great. So was the creation of the earth as their mortal dwelling place.

PRAYER CENTERS OUR ATTITUDES

Watch ye therefore, and pray always, that ye may be accounted worthy to escape all these things that shall come to pass, and to stand before the Son of man.

LUKE 21:36

If we are called to positions of leadership, we are accountable to the Savior for the acts we perform in that office. Those actions are shaped by attitudes, and attitudes are elevated while lowering our heads in humble prayer. . . .

Praying helps us to face trials in life. Prayer centers our attitudes precisely. With that focus we do not wander to the right or left through land mined with traps of temptation.

MEMBER MISSIONARIES

Wherefore, you are called to cry repentance unto this people. And if it so be that you should labor all your days in crying repentance unto this people, and bring, save it be one soul unto me, how great shall be your joy with him in the kingdom of my Father!

DOCTRINE AND COVENANTS 18:14–15

Most have not been and may never be full-time missionaries. But all can be member missionaries. . . . Each member can be an example of the believers. . . . Your good works will be evident to others. The light of the Lord can beam from your eyes. With that radiance, you had better prepare for questions. . . .

Let your response be warm and joyful. And let your response be relevant to that individual. Remember, he or she is also a child of God, that very God who dearly wants that person to qualify for eternal life and return to Him one day. You may be the very one to open the door to his or her salvation and understanding of the doctrine of Christ.

REVERENT SACRAMENT

And as they were eating, Jesus took bread, and
blessed it, and brake it, and gave it to the disciples,
and said, Take, eat; this is my body.

MATTHEW 26:26

Ask yourself, "What do I think of when I partake of the sacrament? Do I really concentrate on the Atonement of Jesus Christ? Do I comprehend the magnitude of His sacrifice and the magnificence of my future as I take upon myself the name of Jesus Christ and resolve to keep His commandments? As His witness, do I worthily partake of the broken bread in remembrance of His broken body? Do I worthily partake of the water, blessed and sanctified to the souls of all those who drink of it, in remembrance of His blood shed for us?" You can recognize progress each week as you thoughtfully, regularly, and worthily partake of the sacrament.

THE SABBATH DAY

*Keep the sabbath day to sanctify it, as the
Lord thy God hath commanded thee.*

DEUTERONOMY 5:12

Once I had the Sabbath day concept figured out, and understood that what I did on Sunday was a sign of my love for God, I realized that just as it wouldn't show my love for Him by operating on Sunday when it could wait until Monday, it also wouldn't show love for God if I let someone die on Sunday who could have been saved. For a cardiovascular surgeon, that scripture was lifesaving for my conscience and my heart.

OBEDIENCE BRINGS JOY

He that covereth his sins shall not prosper: but whoso
confesseth and forsaketh them shall have mercy.

PROVERBS 28:13

Knowing we are created as children of God, and by Him given agency to choose, we must also know that we are accountable to Him. He has defined the truth and prescribed commandments. Obedience to His law will bring us joy. Disobedience of those commandments is defined as sin. While we live in a world that seems increasingly reluctant to designate dishonorable deeds as sinful, a scripture so warns: "Fools make a mock at sin: but among the righteous there is favour" (Proverbs 14:9).

REAR CHILDREN IN LOVE

And all thy children shall be taught of the Lord;
and great shall be the peace of thy children.

3 NEPHI 22:13

We need parents . . . who can rear their children in love. Please teach your children to love and honor their parents, and make it easy for them to love you. Occasionally children need correction. Please give it quietly and privately. But in public, praise them and build their self-confidence. There is no place in the Lord's plan for physical abuse of any kind. That is Satan's way. The Lord's ways are much better!

THE FATHER AND THE SON

And because he dwelleth in flesh he shall be called the Son of God, and having subjected the flesh to the will of the Father, being the Father and the Son—the Father, because he was conceived by the power of God; and the Son, because of the flesh; thus becoming the Father and Son.

MOSIAH 15:2–3

Though separate from His Heavenly Father in both body and spirit, Jesus is one with His Father in power and purpose. . . . Some may wonder why the Son is occasionally referred to as "the Father." The designation used for any man can vary. Every man is a son but may also be called father, brother, uncle, or grandfather, depending on his circumstance. So we must not allow ourselves to become confused regarding divine identity, purpose, or doctrine. Because Jesus was our Creator, He is known in scripture as "the Father of all things" (Mosiah 7:27). . . .

We comprehend that distinction [between the Father and Son] well when we pray to our Heavenly Father in the name of His Son, Jesus Christ. And as we do so regularly, we honor our heavenly and earthly parentage, just as Jesus honored His—as the Son of God.

GOD LIVES

*For I know that my redeemer liveth, and that he
shall stand at the latter day upon the earth.*

JOB 19:25

God lives! He has not died or gone on vacation, nor has He lost interest in His children. There is no direction in which we can turn, no philosophical shield behind which we can hide, no parliamentary edict we can assert which will evade God's exacting gaze or excuse us from obedience to His commandments. . . .

The Lord has taught plainly and repeatedly that if people keep His commandments they will prosper. . . . We can correctly conclude that if we want favorable conditions for our fellow citizens—even protection from pestilence and plagues—our people must be free to learn the commandments of God and obey them.

YOKED WITH
JESUS CHRIST

Take my yoke upon you, and learn of me; for I am meek and lowly in heart: and ye shall find rest unto your souls.

MATTHEW 11:29

Disciples do not flirt with danger at the jagged edge of disaster. Experienced mountain climbers do not lean toward the dangerous edge but toward safety, with ropes and other safeguards to secure them to those they trust. So it is with us. When we climb mountainous challenges of life, we should lean toward our Master and be yoked with Him, clinging tightly to the iron rod of the gospel, to family, and to trusted friends. . . .

Race, nationality, occupation, or other interests need not stand in the way. All can look to the Lord. All can place Him first in their lives.

A FAMILY MATTER

*Behold, I will send you Elijah the prophet before the coming of
the great and dreadful day of the Lord: And he shall turn the
heart of the fathers to the children, and the heart of the children
to their fathers, lest I come and smite the earth with a curse.*

MALACHI 4:5–6

Any discussion of family responsibilities to prepare
for exaltation would be incomplete if we included only
mother, father, and children. What about grandparents
and other ancestors? The Lord has revealed that we
cannot become perfect without them; neither can they
without us be made perfect (see Doctrine and Covenants
128:15). Sealing ordinances are essential to exaltation.
A wife needs to be sealed to her husband; children need
to be sealed to their parents; and we all need to be connected with our ancestors. . . .

This life is the time to prepare for salvation and exaltation. In God's eternal plan, salvation is an individual
matter; exaltation is a family matter. . . . The final responsibility to prepare for salvation and exaltation rests
upon each person, accountable for individual agency,
acting in one's own family.

INCALCULABLE WORTH

And as all have not faith, seek ye diligently and teach one another words of wisdom; yea, seek ye out of the best books words of wisdom; seek learning, even by study and also by faith.

DOCTRINE AND COVENANTS 88:118

You really don't know what you know until you endeavor to teach it. And while you teach diligently, you may learn more fully the fundamentals that pertain to your field of interest. Expose yourselves broadly to the great literature of other eras and of other disciplines. In them you will find teachings of incalculable worth.

GOOD AND EVIL

Blessed are they which do hunger and thirst after
righteousness: for they shall be filled.

MATTHEW 5:6

Our more important choices are those between right and wrong. Inasmuch as good and evil forces do exist in the world, it is not surprising that they compete most keenly in the arena of appetite—yes, in each of our many physical appetites. Many choices have moral implications. There are good and there are evil things for us to see. There are good and evil things to which we may listen. There are good and evil things that we may feel, eat, drink, or otherwise allow into our bodies. I would define moral in terms of commandments of God. We are moral if we are in line with direction He has given.

THREE QUESTIONS

*God conversed with men, and made known unto
them the plan of redemption, which had been
prepared from the foundation of the world.*

ALMA 12:30

I would suggest three questions you might ask yourself
as you consider your options. Whether they are once-in-
a-lifetime or routine daily decisions, serious reflection on
these three questions will help clarify your thinking. . . .
They are:

"Who am I?"

"Why am I here?"

"Where am I going?"

Truthful answers to these three questions will remind
you of important anchors and unchanging principles.

As you consider these fundamental questions, it will
become clear that decisions you first thought to be purely
personal virtually always impact the lives of others. In
answering these questions, then, you must be mindful
of the broader circle of family and friends who will be
affected by the consequences of your choice.

HARMONY IN MARRIAGE

Live joyfully with the wife whom thou lovest all the days of the life of thy vanity, which he hath given thee under the sun.

ECCLESIASTES 9:9

Each marriage starts with two built-in handicaps. It involves two imperfect people. Happiness can come to them only through their earnest effort. Just as harmony comes from an orchestra only when its members make a concerted effort, so harmony in marriage also requires a concerted effort. That effort will succeed if each partner will minimize personal demands and maximize actions of loving selflessness. . . .

Harmony in marriage comes only when one esteems the welfare of his or her spouse among the highest of priorities. When that really happens, a celestial marriage becomes a reality, bringing great joy in this life and in the life to come.

SEPTEMBER

———

For God is not the author of
confusion, but of peace, as in
all churches of the saints.

1 CORINTHIANS 14:33

TRUE REPENTANCE

And now behold, I ask of you, my brethren of the church, have ye spiritually been born of God? Have ye received his image in your countenances? Have ye experienced this mighty change in your hearts?

ALMA 5:14

Can we begin to see the breadth and depth of what the Lord is giving to us when He offers us the gift *to repent*? He invites us to change our minds, and our knowledge. Repentance is a resplendent gift. It is a process never to be feared. It is a gift for us to receive with joy and to use—even embrace—day after day as we seek to become more like our Savior.

King Lamoni's father caught a glimpse of what lay ahead for those who believed in Christ and followed Him. He declared that he would give away all his sins for the privilege of knowing the Lord. True repentance is not an event. It is a never-ending privilege. It is fundamental to progression and having peace of mind, comfort, and joy.

THE GATHERING

And verily I say unto you, I give unto you a sign, that ye may know the time when these things shall be about to take place—that I shall gather in, from their long dispersion, my people, O house of Israel, and shall establish again among them my Zion.

3 NEPHI 21:1

A necessary prelude to that Second Coming is the long-awaited gathering of scattered Israel. This doctrine of the gathering is one of the important teachings of The Church of Jesus Christ of Latter-day Saints. . . .

We not only teach this doctrine, but we participate in it. We do so as we help to gather the elect of the Lord on both sides of the veil. As part of the planned destiny of the earth and its inhabitants, our kindred dead are to be redeemed. Mercifully, the invitation to "come unto Christ" (Jacob 1:7) can also be extended to those who died without a knowledge of the gospel. Part of their preparation, however, requires the earthly efforts of others. We gather pedigree charts, create family group sheets, and do temple work vicariously to gather individuals unto the Lord and into their families.

RISE ABOVE

If thou art called to pass through tribulation; . . .
Know thou, my son, that all these things shall give thee
experience, and shall be for thy good. The Son of Man hath
descended below them all. Art thou greater than he?

DOCTRINE AND COVENANTS 122:5, 7–8

Difficult days are ahead for all mankind. Sin is on the increase. We live in a time of wars and rumors of wars. The Church and its members will come under attack and endure persecution.

Jesus descended below all things in order to rise above all things. He expects us to follow His example. Yoked with Him, we can rise above all challenges, no matter how difficult they may be.

EFFORT AND OBEDIENCE

Behold, the Lord requireth the heart and a willing
mind; and the willing and obedient shall eat the
good of the land of Zion in these last days.

DOCTRINE AND COVENANTS 64:34

Mountains are not easy to climb. Then, as now, the Lord called His disciples to climb mountains to emphasize the efficacy of effort and obedience. He will ask the same of you, figuratively and possibly literally, also.

Jesus Christ . . . used a mountain to emphasize effort in His Sermon on the Mount. While [Jesus was] speaking near the northern shore of the Sea of Galilee, His disciples were commanded to be perfect even as their Father in Heaven. They were taught the principles of prayer. They were commanded to seek first the kingdom of God and His righteousness. The Lord promised salvation to those who followed His example in doing the will of His Father.

SPIRITUAL DEVELOPMENT

Behold, it has been made known unto me by an angel, that
the spirits of all men, as soon as they are departed from this
mortal body, yea, the spirits of all men, whether they be good
or evil, are taken home to that God who gave them life.

ALMA 40:11

Important as is the body, it serves as a tabernacle for one's eternal spirit. Our spirits existed in the premortal realm and will continue to live after the body dies. The spirit provides the body with animation and personality. In this life and in the next, spirit and body, when joined together, become a living soul of supernal worth.

Because one's spirit is so important, its development is of eternal consequence. It is strengthened as we communicate in humble prayer with our loving Heavenly Father.

DO BETTER AND
BE BETTER

Therefore turn thou to thy God: keep mercy and judgment, and wait on thy God continually.

HOSEA 12:6

Whether you are diligently moving along the covenant path, have slipped or stepped from the covenant path, or can't even see the path from where you are now, I plead with you to repent. Experience the strengthening power of daily repentance—of doing and being a little better each day.

When we choose to repent, we choose to change! We allow the Savior to transform us into the best version of ourselves. We choose to grow spiritually and receive joy—the joy of redemption in Him. When we choose to repent, we choose to become more like Jesus Christ!

PERFECTION IS PENDING

Behold, ye are little children and ye cannot bear all things now;
ye must grow in grace and in the knowledge of the truth.

DOCTRINE AND COVENANTS 50:40

Brothers and sisters, let us do the best we can and try to improve each day. When our imperfections appear, we can keep trying to correct them. We can be more forgiving of flaws in ourselves and among those we love. We can be comforted and forbearing. . . .

We need not be dismayed if our earnest efforts toward perfection now seem so arduous and endless. Perfection is pending. It can come in full only after the Resurrection and only through the Lord. It awaits all who love Him and keep His commandments. It includes thrones, kingdoms, principalities, powers, and dominions. It is the end for which we are to endure. It is the eternal perfection that God has in store for each of us.

AN INDIVIDUAL MATTER

I the Lord search the heart, I try the reins, even to give every man according to his ways, and according to the fruit of his doings.

JEREMIAH 17:10

Some years ago I met with a tribal king in Africa. When he realized that he was being taught by an Apostle of the Lord, he was deeply moved. He said that throngs of his people would be baptized if he were to give them such a mandate. I thanked him for his kindness but explained that the Lord does not work in that way.

The development of faith in the Lord is an individual matter. Repentance is also an individual matter. Only as an individual can one be baptized and receive the Holy Ghost. Each of us is born individually; likewise, each of us is "born again" individually (John 3:3). Salvation is an individual matter.

THE GIFT OF AGENCY

And now remember, remember, my brethren, that whosoever
perisheth, perisheth unto himself; and whosoever doeth
iniquity, doeth it unto himself; for behold, ye are free; ye
are permitted to act for yourselves; for behold, God hath
given unto you a knowledge and he hath made you free.

HELAMAN 14:30

We reach out in love to family, friends, and neighbors, regardless of nationality or creed, who suffer addiction. . . . The solution to this problem ultimately is neither governmental nor institutional. Nor is it a question of legality. It is a matter of individual choice and commitment. Agency must be understood. The importance of the will in making crucial choices must be known. Then steps toward relief can follow.

Agency, or the power to choose, was ours as spirit children of our Creator before the world was. It is a gift from God, nearly as precious as life itself.

Often, however, agency is misunderstood. While we are free to choose, once we have made those choices, we are tied to the consequences of those choices.

TRUE UNDERSHEPHERDS

*Therefore, fear not, little flock; do good; let earth
and hell combine against you, for if ye are built
upon my rock, they cannot prevail.*

DOCTRINE AND COVENANTS 6:34

Personal security through the travails of life cannot be guaranteed by wealth, fame, or governmental programs. But it can come from doing the will of the Lord, whose instructions are given to bring spiritual protection to His Saints. His merciful commandments, with undergirding and overarching power to sustain all natural law, tenderly allow gentle hands to guard His children well.

The Good Shepherd lovingly cares for all sheep of His fold, and we are His true undershepherds. Our privilege is to bear His love and to add our own love to friends and neighbors—feeding, tending, and nurturing them—as the Savior would have us do. By so doing, we evidence one of the godly characteristics of His restored Church upon the earth.

THE PRINCE OF PEACE

He healeth the broken in heart,
and bindeth up their wounds.

PSALM 147:3

Peace can come to those who are not feeling well. Some bodies are wounded. Others ache spiritually because of missing loved ones or other emotional trauma. Brothers and sisters, peace can come to your soul as you build faith in the Prince of Peace. . . .

Peace can come to one who suffers in sorrow. Whether sorrow stems from a mistake or a sin, all the Lord requires is real repentance. . . .

Peace can come to all who choose to walk in the ways of the Master. His invitation is expressed in three loving words: "Come, follow me" (Luke 18:22).

A MORE EXCELLENT HOPE

And I also remember that thou hast said that thou hast prepared a house for man, yea, even among the mansions of thy Father, in which man might have a more excellent hope; wherefore man must hope, or he cannot receive an inheritance in the place which thou hast prepared.

ETHER 12:32

A more excellent hope is mightier than a wistful wish. Hope, fortified by faith and charity, forges a force as strong as steel. Hope becomes an anchor to the soul. To this anchor the faithful can cling, securely tethered to the Lord. Satan, on the other hand, would have us cast away that anchor and drift with the ebb tide of despair. If we will cling to the anchor of hope, it will be our safeguard *forever*.

AUTHORITY TO BLESS

Lay your hands upon the sick, and they shall recover. Return not till I, the Lord, shall send you. Be patient in affliction. Ask, and ye shall receive; knock, and it shall be opened unto you.

DOCTRINE AND COVENANTS 66:9

To bear the priesthood means you have a personal responsibility to magnify your calling. Let each opportunity to serve help to develop your power in the priesthood. In your personal grooming, follow the example of the living prophets. Doing so gives silent expression that you truly comprehend the importance of "the Holy Priesthood, after the Order of the Son of God" (Doctrine and Covenants 107:3).

When you brethren have an opportunity to exercise the Melchizedek Priesthood, ponder what you are to do. When you lay hands upon the head of another, you are not offering a prayer, which of course requires no authority. You are authorized to set apart, to ordain, to bless, and to speak in the name of the Lord.

A HOUSE OF LEARNING

Organize yourselves; prepare every needful thing;
and establish a house, even a house of prayer, a house
of fasting, a house of faith, a house of learning, a
house of glory, a house of order, a house of God.

DOCTRINE AND COVENANTS 88:119

Each temple is a house of learning. There we are taught in the Master's way. His way differs from modes of others. His way is ancient and rich with symbolism. We can learn much by pondering the reality for which each symbol stands. Teachings of the temple are beautifully simple and simply beautiful. They are understood by the humble, yet they can excite the intellect of the brightest minds.

Spiritual preparation is enhanced by study. I like to recommend that members going to the temple for the first time read short explanatory paragraphs in the Bible Dictionary, listed under seven topics: "Anoint," "Atonement," "Christ," "Covenant," "Fall of Adam," "Sacrifices," and "Temple." Doing so will provide a firm foundation.

LIFE EVERLASTING

And this is the record, that God hath given to us eternal life, and this life is in his Son. He that hath the Son hath life; and he that hath not the Son of God hath not life.

1 JOHN 5:11–12

Another gift from our Savior is actually a promise—a promise of *life everlasting*. This does not mean simply living for a really, really, really long time. Everyone will live forever after death, regardless of the kingdom or glory for which they may qualify. Everyone will be resurrected and experience *immortality*. But eternal life is so much more than a designation of time. Eternal life is the kind and quality of life that Heavenly Father and His Beloved Son live. When the Father offers us everlasting life, He is saying in essence, "If you choose to follow my Son—if your *desire* is *really* to become more like Him—then in time you may live as we live and preside over worlds and kingdoms as we do."

THE LORD'S LAMBS

Nevertheless, the people of the church did have great joy . . .
because of the church of God, which had been established
among them. And they did fellowship one with another,
and did rejoice one with another, and did have great joy.

HELAMAN 6:3

I hope that each ward council would conscientiously care for each previous lamb in the fold of God. He expects each bishop to preside over the sheep of His fold. We are to care for the Lords' little lambs. We tend them; we feed them. We care for our brothers and sisters. We care for our friends and neighbors. Let us consider them name by name in our ward councils.

COME TO KNOW

Verily, thus saith the Lord: It shall come to pass that every soul who forsaketh his sins and cometh unto me, and calleth on my name, and obeyeth my voice, and keepeth my commandments, shall see my face and know that I am.

DOCTRINE AND COVENANTS 93:1

Will you establish priorities to help you make your choices in life?

Your choices will not all be between good and evil. Many will be choices between two good options. Not all truths are created equal. So you will need to establish priorities.

In your pursuit of knowledge, know that *the very most* important truth you can learn comes from the Lord. In His intercessory prayer to His Father, the Savior Himself confirmed this. He said: "This is life eternal, that they might know thee the only true God, and Jesus Christ, whom thou hast sent" (John 17:3). Above everything else you are seeking to learn, seek to know God, your Heavenly Father, and His Son, Jesus Christ. Come to know Them and love Them as I do.

TO BE SAVED AND EXALTED

Therefore, all things shall be restored to their proper order, every thing to its natural frame—mortality raised to immortality, corruption to incorruption—raised to endless happiness to inherit the kingdom of God, or to endless misery to inherit the kingdom of the devil, the one on one hand, the other on the other.

ALMA 41:4

To be saved—or to gain salvation—means to be saved from physical and spiritual death. Because of the Resurrection of Jesus Christ, all people will be resurrected and saved from physical death. People may also be saved from individual spiritual death through the Atonement of Jesus Christ, by their faith in Him, by living in obedience to the laws and ordinances of His gospel, and by serving Him.

To be exalted—or to gain exaltation—refers to the highest state of happiness and glory in the celestial realm. These blessings can come to us after we leave this frail and mortal existence. The time to prepare for our eventual salvation and exaltation is now.

PROPHETIC COUNSEL

For his word ye shall receive, as if from mine own mouth, in all patience and faith.

DOCTRINE AND COVENANTS 21:5

Some revelations have been given for unique circumstances, such as Noah's building of the ark or the necessity for prophets like Moses, Lehi, and Brigham to lead their followers in arduous travel. God's long-established pattern of teaching His children through prophets assures us that He will bless each prophet and that He will bless those who heed prophetic counsel.

A desire to follow the prophet requires much effort because the natural man knows very little of God and even less of His prophet.

BLESSINGS OF ABRAHAMIC COVENANT

And he that receiveth my Father receiveth my Father's kingdom; therefore all that my Father hath shall be given unto him.

DOCTRINE AND COVENANTS 84:38

How do you obtain your *blessings?* How can you qualify for eternal blessings—even "all that [the] Father hath"? With your identity preserved and your priorities properly honored, our Father's blessings will flow to you by virtue of the holy priesthood. . . .

You can lay claim to all the blessings of the Abrahamic covenant, destined to be fulfilled in these latter days. Blessings and responsibilities once extended to other nations have now been given to us. Patriarchal blessings reveal our linkage to the great patriarchs Abraham, Isaac, and Jacob. *We are* the seed of Abraham through whom all the nations of the earth will be blessed. That identity merits our precious priority, which in turn brings to us the blessings of heaven.

The ultimate blessings of the Abrahamic covenant are conferred in a holy temple.

COMMITMENT KEEPING

Commit thy way unto the Lord; trust also in him; and he shall bring it to pass.

PSALM 37:5

Commitment keeping prepares a person for covenant keeping. The gospel of Jesus Christ includes the making and keeping of sacred covenants, the first of which is the covenant of baptism. The act of baptism does not wash sin away. Thanks to the Atonement, the effects of sin depart when one faithfully keeps the baptismal covenant to follow the Lord Jesus Christ.

SERVING HIM

*Let all the house of Israel know assuredly, that God hath
made that same Jesus, whom ye have crucified, both Lord and
Christ. Now when they heard this, they were pricked in their
heart. . . . Then Peter said unto them, Repent, and be baptized
every one of you in the name of Jesus Christ for the remission
of sins, and ye shall receive the gift of the Holy Ghost.*

ACTS 2:36–38

Embracing [the Savior's] teachings—and helping others do so—is the great work of these latter days. That is why we have missionaries; that is why we have temples—to bring the fullest blessings of the Atonement to faithful children of God. That is why we respond to our own calls from the Lord. When we comprehend His voluntary Atonement, any sense of sacrifice on our part becomes completely overshadowed by a profound sense of gratitude for the privilege of serving Him.

RESURRECTION IS REQUISITE

If a man die, shall he live again? all the days of my appointed time will I wait, till my change come.

JOB 14:14

Resurrection is requisite for eternal perfection. Thanks to the Atonement of Jesus Christ, our bodies, corruptible in mortality, will become incorruptible. Our physical frames, now subject to disease, death, and decay, will acquire immortal glory. Presently sustained by the blood of life and ever aging, our bodies will be sustained by spirit and become changeless and beyond the bounds of death.

NO LIMIT

For I have given you an example, that ye
should do as I have done to you.

JOHN 13:15

The Lord's . . . exemplary life constituted His mortal ministry. It included His teachings, parables, and sermons. It encompassed His miracles, His loving kindness, humility, and His long-suffering towards the children of men. . . .

Wonderful as His ministerial acts were, they were not and are still not unique to Him.

There is no limit to the number of people who may follow the example of Jesus. Similar acts have been done by His prophets and apostles or others among His authorized servants. Many have endured persecution for His sake. Many of you brothers and sisters have earnestly strived—even at a terrible price—to emulate the Lord's example.

That is how it should be. That is His hope for us.

COMMANDED TO SACRIFICE

The sacrifices of God are a broken spirit: a broken and a contrite heart, O God, thou wilt not despise.

PSALM 51:17

When Jesus Christ came to the earth, He fulfilled the promised role as He became the ultimate sacrificial lamb. His Atonement brought about a greater destiny and a nobler concept for us. We are still commanded to sacrifice, but not by shedding blood of animals. Our highest sense of sacrifice is achieved as we make ourselves more sacred or holy.

This we do by our obedience to the commandments of God. Thus, the laws of obedience and sacrifice are indelibly intertwined. Consider the commandments to obey the Word of Wisdom, to keep the Sabbath day holy, to pay an honest tithe. As we comply with these and other commandments, something wonderful happens to us. We become disciplined! We become disciples! We become more sacred and holy—like our Lord!

SIMPLE DOCTRINE

A new commandment I give unto you, That ye love one another; as I have loved you, that ye also love one another.

JOHN 13:34

Our doctrine is not complicated, convoluted, or complex. It is so simple—love God and love your neighbor. Maybe it is revelation; maybe it is just being obedient to those two great commandments. It is really reduced to the simplest terms when we are talking about loving, serving, caring, and making life better for people. Isn't that what the gospel is all about? We want people to have a better way of life.

FINEST
LEADERSHIP SKILLS

Our kings and our leaders were mighty men in the faith of
the Lord; and they taught the people the ways of the Lord.

JAROM 1:7

Your responsibility to the Lord to help gather the elect out of the moral chaos and swirling preponderance of sin in our day is no small undertaking. Lucifer and his minions are using every form of technology and communication to spread lies about life and about the true source of happiness. Thus, to do what you came to earth to do will require the finest leadership skills your generation can muster.

Thankfully, we have superb models to follow. While the world may look to the considerable leadership abilities of men and women such as Napoleon, Joan of Arc, George Washington, Mahatma Gandhi, Mother Teresa, and others, I believe that the finest leaders to have walked the earth are the prophets of God.

MASTER YOUR WEAKNESS

*Because thou hast seen thy weakness thou shalt be made
strong, even unto the sitting down in the place which
I have prepared in the mansions of my Father.*

ETHER 12:37

Please don't be discouraged or depressed by your short-comings. No one is without weakness. That is part of the divine plan—to determine if you will master that weakness, or let the weakness master you. Proper diagnosis is essential to proper treatment. . . .

But wishing for strength won't make it so. It takes faith and work to shore up a weakened cord of integrity.

That process of repair you know as *repentance,* and, mercifully, you don't have to begin it alone. Help can be received through counsel with trusted parents and Church leaders. But their aid is more likely to be help-ful if you seek it, not merely to satisfy a formality, but with "real intent" to reform yourself and come closer to Christ. He is the Ultimate Physician. Real faith in Him will provide real relief—and glorious rewards.

SEEK THE LORD

The Lord is good unto them that wait for
him, to the soul that seeketh him.

LAMENTATIONS 3:25

My dear brothers and sisters, you have as much access to the mind and will of the Lord for your own life as we Apostles do for His Church. Just as the Lord requires *us* to seek and ponder, fast and pray, and study and wrestle with difficult questions, He requires *you* to do the same as you seek answers to your own questions.

You can learn to hear the voice of the Lord through the whisperings of the Holy Ghost. As helpful as Google, Twitter, and Facebook may seem, they simply do not provide answers to your most important questions!

. . . You can know the mind and will of the Lord for your own life. You do not have to wonder if you are where the Lord needs you to be or if you are doing what He needs you to do. You can know! The Holy Ghost "will tell you all things what ye should do" (2 Nephi 32:3).

GOD'S COMMANDMENTS

And hereby we do know that we know him,
if we keep his commandments.

1 JOHN 2:3

The Ten Commandments . . . comprise the great moral code of our society. . . . We had better memorize them, just as we have learned the alphabet and multiplication tables.

The first four pertain to our relationship with God; the remaining six pertain to our relationships with fellow human beings. As we consider each of them, we might reflect not only on God the Giver, but on Satan the opposer as well. All good in the world comes from God; all evil stems from Satan. As the evil one, he fights against each commandment and creates conflict in the minds of mortals at each of the ten. He further hopes that conflicting thoughts will be followed by deeds counter to divine commandments, thereby enslaving our souls and denying us blessings from heaven.

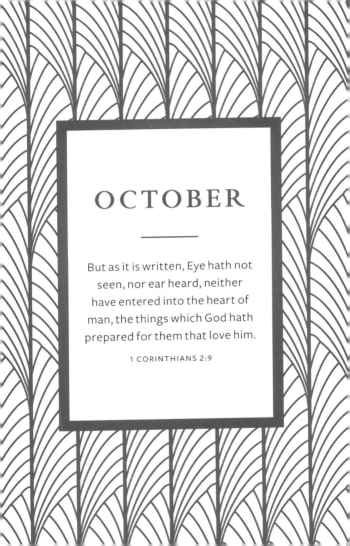

OCTOBER

But as it is written, Eye hath not seen, nor ear heard, neither have entered into the heart of man, the things which God hath prepared for them that love him.

1 CORINTHIANS 2:9

HOPE IN REVELATION

We believe all that God has revealed, all that He does now reveal, and we believe that He will yet reveal many great and important things pertaining to the Kingdom of God.

ARTICLES OF FAITH 1:9

I am optimistic about the future. It will be filled with opportunities for each of us to progress, contribute, and take the gospel to every corner of the earth. But I am also not naïve about the days ahead. We live in a world that is complex and increasingly contentious. The constant availability of social media and a 24-hour news cycle bombard us with relentless messages. If we are to have any hope sifting through the myriad of voices and the philosophies of men that attack truth, we must learn to receive revelation.

THE SAVIOR'S POWER

And also my soul delighteth in the covenants of the
Lord . . . ; yea, my soul delighteth in his grace, and
in his justice, and power, and mercy in the great
and eternal plan of deliverance from death.

2 NEPHI 11:5

Every woman and every man who makes covenants with God and keeps those covenants, and who participates worthily in priesthood ordinances, has direct access to the power of God. Those who are endowed in the house of the Lord receive a gift of God's priesthood power by virtue of their covenant, along with a gift of knowledge to know how to draw upon that power.

The heavens are just as open to *women* who are endowed with God's power flowing from their priesthood covenants as they are to men who bear the priesthood. I pray that truth will register upon each of your hearts because I believe it will change your life. Sisters, you have the right to draw liberally upon the Savior's power to help your family and others you love.

OUR KINDRED DEAD

These are principles in relation to the dead and the living that cannot be lightly passed over, as pertaining to our salvation. For their salvation is necessary and essential to our salvation, as Paul says concerning the fathers—that they without us cannot be made perfect—neither can we without our dead be made perfect.

DOCTRINE AND COVENANTS 128:15

Principles of agency pertain on both sides of the veil. There, in postmortal realms, personal choice and accountability will be of paramount importance. Not all will accept these ordinances. Not all that would choose to do so may be worthy to receive them. Scriptures indicate that individual faith, repentance, and obedience will be required to consummate this vicarious work.

Here, on this side of the veil, there are limitations of available time and temples. This means that choosing to identify and perform ordinances for *our own kindred* should receive our highest priority. The spirit of Elijah will inspire individual members of the Church to link their generations, rather than submit lists of people or popular personalities to whom they are unrelated.

ONE BODY
IN CHRIST

*So we, being many, are one body in Christ,
and every one members one of another.*

ROMANS 12:5

Just as we need each part of our body, the Lord has need of every member. And every member also needs the Lord. . . . You work together in your quorums and ward councils to accomplish the rescue of precious souls, one by one. Just as a heart needs the power of each of its muscle fibers working together in unison, so we need every member adding his or her power as part of the heart of the Church.

ORDINANCES OF SALVATION AND EXALTATION

Now I praise you, brethren, that ye remember me in all things, and keep the ordinances, as I delivered them to you.

1 CORINTHIANS 11:2

The ordinances of salvation and exaltation are part of the eternal plan of God. The ordinances of baptism and the gift of the Holy Ghost are initiatory ordinances. They are linked with the invitation to come unto Christ. They enable one to enter the "strait and narrow path" (2 Nephi 31:18–19), which leads to the ordinances of exaltation and blessings of the holy temple. There a wife may be sealed to her husband, children can be sealed to their parents, and families may be prepared to endure to the end and be together forever to enjoy the blessings of eternal life.

HEAVENS ARE OPEN

*And they shall also be crowned with blessings from above, yea,
and with commandments not a few, and with revelations in
their time—they that are faithful and diligent before me.*

DOCTRINE AND COVENANTS 59:4

Undergirding Church history were revelations received
and recorded by Joseph Smith. He protected and preserved them. Explicitly, he followed instructions received
in them. . . . The importance and relevance of these revelations lies in the fact that the heavens are open. It is in
the fact that God *lives,* that His Beloved Son Jesus is
the *living* Christ, and that they direct the affairs of His
Church by revelation to *living* prophets.

This access to revelation is not limited to presidents,
prophets, and apostles. All of God's children are invited
to receive personal revelation. . . .

Joseph Smith became great *because* of revelation.
Without revelation, Joseph would merely have been just
Joseph. Gratefully, we, too, can become greater than we
otherwise would be—by receiving and responding to
personal revelation.

THE LORD'S COVENANT PATH

That thou shouldest enter into covenant with the Lord thy God, and into his oath, which the Lord thy God maketh with thee this day: That he may establish thee to day for a people unto himself, and that he may be unto thee a God, as he hath said unto thee.

DEUTERONOMY 29:12–13

What is the key to loving as He loves, forgiving as He forgives, repenting to become more like Him, and ultimately living with Him and our Heavenly Father?

The key is to make and keep sacred covenants. We *choose* to live and progress on the Lord's covenant path and to stay on it. It is not a complicated way. It is *the* way to true joy in this life and eternal life beyond.

LOCATION OF THE LORD'S MINISTRY

For the Lord shall comfort Zion: he will comfort all her waste places; and he will make her wilderness like Eden, and her desert like the garden of the Lord; joy and gladness shall be found therein, thanksgiving, and the voice of melody.

ISAIAH 51:3

Have you ever wondered why the Lord chose to accomplish His mortal ministry in the exact location that He did? He created the earth. In His divine role, He could have selected any portion of this bounteous planet to accomplish His mission. He could have selected the beautiful islands of the sea with their lush vegetation and breathtaking beauty. He could have chosen the scenery of Switzerland or Scandinavia, or He could have preferred to walk upon the acres of Africa or Australia.

Instead, He selected the land with places stark and arid, but made holy by His presence there. He did so for many reasons, including His desire to teach with geographical visual aids, and to fulfill scripture.

THE FULL POWER
OF THE GOSPEL

And he has translated the book, even that part which I have commanded him, and as your Lord and your God liveth it is true.

DOCTRINE AND COVENANTS 17:6

The Book of Mormon provides the fullest and most authoritative understanding of the Atonement of Jesus Christ to be found anywhere. It teaches what it really means to be born again. From the Book of Mormon we learn about the gathering of scattered Israel. We know why we are here on earth. These and other truths are more powerfully and persuasively taught in the Book of Mormon than in any other book. The full power of the gospel of Jesus Christ is contained in the Book of Mormon. Period.

NOURISHING
THE SPIRIT

*But the manifestation of the Spirit is given
to every man to profit withal.*
1 CORINTHIANS 12:7

The attributes by which we shall be judged one day are all spiritual. These include love, virtue, integrity, compassion, and service to others. Your spirit, coupled with and housed in your body, is able to develop and manifest these attributes in ways that are vital to your eternal progression. Spiritual progress is attained through the steps of faith, repentance, baptism, the gift of the Holy Ghost, and enduring to the end, including the endowment and sealing ordinances of the holy temple.

Just as the body requires daily food for survival, the spirit needs nourishment as well. The spirit is nurtured by eternal truth.

WE BELIEVE
IN ANGELS

*I will go before your face. I will be on your right hand
and on your left, and my Spirit shall be in your hearts,
and mine angels round about you, to bear you up.*

DOCTRINE AND COVENANTS 84:88

Often our members are "angels" to neighbors in need. Home teachers and visiting teachers, as ordinary people, frequently render service that seems angelic to grateful recipients. Young people who quietly leave homemade goodies on a doorstep or two experience the joy of anonymous service to others. And I am among the many who have often referred to the loving acts of an "angel mother" or an "angel wife," or the priceless love of "angel children."

Do we believe in angels? *Yes!* We believe in angels—heavenly messengers—seen and unseen; and earthly angels who know *whom* to help and *how* to help. Gospel messengers, or angels, can include ordinary people like you and me.

May angels, known and unknown, serve you and protect you along life's perilous journey.

THE CHURCH OF JESUS CHRIST

For thus shall my church be called in the last days, even
The Church of Jesus Christ of Latter-day Saints.

DOCTRINE AND COVENANTS 115:4

The true name of the Church is The Church of Jesus Christ of Latter-day Saints. It is the reestablished original Church of Jesus Christ. When He walked upon the earth, He organized His Church. He called Apostles, Seventies, and other leaders to whom He gave priesthood authority to act in His name. After Christ and His Apostles passed away, men changed the ordinances and doctrine. The original Church and the priesthood were lost. After the Dark Ages, and under the direction of Heavenly Father, Jesus Christ brought back His Church. Now it lives again, restored and functioning under His divine direction.

NO HOLLOW HOPE

He maketh wars to cease unto the end of the earth; he breaketh
the bow, and cutteth the spear in sunder; he burneth the
chariot in the fire. Be still, and know that I am God: I will
be exalted among the heathen, I will be exalted in the earth.
The Lord of hosts is with us; the God of Jacob is our refuge.

PSALM 46:9–11

Obedience to divine law provides the potential for international peace. Peace among neighbors and nations need not be merely a hollow hope. Feelings of brotherhood among men can be attained only as they acknowledge the fatherhood of God.

THE DOCTRINE
OF CHRIST

*Wherefore, do the things which I have told you I have
seen that your Lord and your Redeemer should do; for,
for this cause have they been shown unto me, that ye
might know the gate by which ye should enter.*

2 NEPHI 31:17

We need to take even greater advantage of the power
of [the Book of Mormon]. Its principal authors and its
inspired translator gave their lives to make it available to
us. We should treat each copy with reverent respect. We
should *not* give it away casually. And we ought *not* to pro-
mote the "speed-reading" of its sacred pages. We should
never make reading the Book of Mormon seem like an
onerous duty, like the gulping of nasty medicine to be
swallowed quickly, and then checked off with finality.

Help the [Saints] to have the thrill of discovering the
divine doctrine of Christ. Help them to feel that sweet,
faith-promoting spirit that comes when one studies the
Book of Mormon, pondering it prayerfully, with a deep
desire to be taught by the Lord Himself. If one studies
the Book of Mormon, heaven will reveal the truth and
deepen one's conversion to the Lord.

THE PROCESS OF REPENTANCE

And they all cried with one voice, saying: Yea, we believe all the words which thou hast spoken unto us; and also, we know of their surety and truth, because of the Spirit of the Lord Omnipotent, which has wrought a mighty change in us, or in our hearts, that we have no more disposition to do evil, but to do good continually.

MOSIAH 5:2

Too many people consider repentance as punishment. . . . But this feeling of being penalized is engendered by Satan. He tries to block us from looking to Jesus Christ, who stands with open arms, hoping and willing to heal, forgive, cleanse, strengthen, purify, and sanctify us. . . . When Jesus asks you and me to "repent," He is inviting us to change our mind, our knowledge, our spirit— even the way we breathe. He is asking us to change the way we love, think, serve, spend our time, treat our wives, teach our children, and even care for our bodies.

Nothing is more liberating, more ennobling, or more crucial to our individual progression than is a regular, daily focus on repentance. Repentance is not an event; it is a process. It is the key to happiness and peace of mind. When coupled with faith, repentance opens our access to the power of the Atonement of Jesus Christ.

THE IMPORTANCE
OF INTEGRITY

Therefore, my son, see that you are merciful unto your brethren;
deal justly, judge righteously, and do good continually; and
if ye do all these things then shall ye receive your reward.

ALMA 41:14

Integrity includes virtue, cleanliness, and honesty. In our world, there is so much of deceit. We learn of cheating in the classrooms, cheating in business, cheating in marriage, and so on. Even though these acts may not be discovered by others, the soul of a cheater suffers. Self-respect vanishes, conscience is warped, and character crumbles.

TRUE LIBERATION

*He that hath no rule over his own spirit is like a
city that is broken down, and without walls.*

PROVERBS 25:28

We can change our behavior. Our very desires can change. How? There is only one way. True change—permanent change—can come only through the healing, cleansing, and enabling power of the Atonement of Jesus Christ. He loves you—each of you! He allows you to access His power as you keep His commandments, eagerly, earnestly, and exactly. It is that simple and certain. The gospel of Jesus Christ *is* a gospel of change!

A strong human spirit with control over appetites of the flesh is master over emotions and passions and not a slave to them. That kind of freedom is as vital to the spirit as oxygen is to the body! Freedom from self-slavery is true liberation!

WHO YOU REALLY ARE

I love the Lord, because he hath heard
my voice and my supplications.

PSALM 116:1

Learn *for yourselves* who you really are. Ask your Heavenly Father, in the name of Jesus Christ, how He feels about you and your mission here on earth. If you ask with real intent, over time the Spirit will whisper the life-changing truth to you. Record those impressions and review them often, and follow through with exactness.

I promise you that when you begin to catch even a glimpse of how your Heavenly Father sees you and what He is counting on you to do for Him, your life will never be the same!

THE GREATEST GIFT OF GOD

Now he which stablisheth us with you in Christ, and
hath anointed us, is God; who hath also sealed us,
and given the earnest of the Spirit in our hearts.

2 CORINTHIANS 1:21–22

In preparing to receive the endowment and other ordinances of the temple, we should understand the sealing authority of the priesthood. Jesus referred to this authority long ago when He taught His Apostles, "Whatsoever thou shalt bind on earth shall be bound in heaven" (Matthew 16:19). That same authority has been restored in these latter days. Just as priesthood is eternal—without beginning or end—so is the effect of priesthood ordinances that bind families together forever.

Temple ordinances, covenants, endowments, and sealings enable individuals to be reconciled with the Lord and families to be sealed beyond the veil of death. Obedience to temple covenants qualifies us for eternal life, the greatest gift of God to man. Eternal life is more than immortality. Eternal life is exaltation in the highest heaven—the kind of life that God lives.

CONSEQUENCES OF SIN

Be not overcome of evil, but overcome evil with good.

ROMANS 12:21

Some people are so easily tempted to lie a little, to cheat a little, to steal a little, or to bear false witness—just a little. You cannot commit a little sin without being subject to the consequences. If you tolerate a little sin today, you tolerate a little more tomorrow, and before long, a cord of integrity is broken. Sequential stress will follow, putting at risk adjacent cords of chastity, virtue, or being true.

TITLES OF JESUS CHRIST

For he hath answered the ends of the law, and he claimeth all those who have faith in him; and they who have faith in him will cleave unto every good thing; wherefore he advocateth the cause of the children of men; and he dwelleth eternally in the heavens.

MORONI 7:28

Study everything Jesus Christ *is* by prayerfully and vigorously seeking to understand what *each* of His various titles and names means for you *personally*. For example, He really is *your* Advocate with the Father. He will take *your* side. He will stand up for *you*. He will speak on *your* behalf, *every time*, as *you* choose to be more like *Him*.

THE FOUNDATION
OF OUR FAITH

Then touched he their eyes, saying,
According to your faith be it unto you.

MATTHEW 9:29

How firm is our foundation? The foundation of this Church was forged long before the world was. It is strong. It is true. It is eternal. The foundation of one's individual faith, if anchored firmly to eternal truth, allows each of us to reach upward with an eternal perspective. That faith will give us hope when there is no hope. It will give us joy here and eternal life hereafter.

THE ANOINTED ONE

How God anointed Jesus of Nazareth with the Holy Ghost and with power: who went about doing good, and healing all that were oppressed of the devil; for God was with him.

ACTS 10:38

Jesus was accorded titles of unique significance. One was the *Messiah,* which in Hebrew means "anointed." The other was the *Christ,* which in the Greek language means "anointed" as well. In our day, as it was in His day, the ordinance of administration to the sick includes anointing with the consecrated oil of the olive. So the next time you witness consecrated oil being anointed on the head of one to be blessed, and these sacred words are said, "I anoint you with this consecrated oil," remember what that original consecration cost. Remember what it meant to all who had ever lived and who ever would yet live. Remember the redemptive power of healing, soothing, and ministering to those in need. Remember, just as the body of the olive, which was pressed for the oil that gave light, so the Savior was pressed. From every pore oozed the lifeblood of our Redeemer.

BLESSINGS FROM OBEDIENCE

*But this thing commanded I them, saying,
Obey my voice, and I will be your God, and ye shall
be my people: and walk ye in all the ways that I have
commanded you, that it may be well unto you.*

JEREMIAH 7:23

Obedience allows God's blessings to flow without constraint. He will bless His obedient children with freedom from bondage and misery. And He will bless them with more light. For example, one keeps the Word of Wisdom knowing that obedience will not only bring freedom from addiction, but it will also add blessings of wisdom and treasures of knowledge.

POWER TO REDEEM

Come now, and let us reason together, saith the Lord:
though your sins be as scarlet, they shall be as white as snow;
though they be red like crimson, they shall be as wool.

ISAIAH 1:18

Jesus is the Christ, our Savior and Redeemer. Our brothers and sisters all need the truth about the Lord. Those who struggle with sin, or who have been victims of the sinful behavior of someone else, or who need help to overcome weakness, or whose faith is wavering—they have an acute need for the redeeming and strengthening power of Jesus Christ in their lives. . . . He is the truth—the Creator of all things. All truth, spiritual and temporal, is part of His gospel. . . .

The Lord Jesus Christ atoned for us. As we repent, He has power to forgive, redeem us from sin, change our hearts, strengthen us, and keep us on the path to our Heavenly Father. This is divine law and absolute truth.

LAND WITH THE TEMPLE

I have hallowed this house, which thou hast built,
to put my name there for ever; and mine eyes
and mine heart shall be there perpetually.

1 KINGS 9:3

The first sacred temple of Jerusalem was constructed on Mount Moriah. At that site, Jesus attended the remodeled second temple. Initially He called it "my Father's house" (John 2:16). There He accomplished the first cleansing of the temple by driving out the money-changers. At the time of the second cleansing, He called it "my house." And He said unto them, "It is written, My house shall be called the house of prayer; but ye have made it a den of thieves" (Matthew 21:13).

Finally and sadly, He called it "your house" when He said in desperation, "Behold, your house is left unto you desolate" (Luke 13:35), and predicted the destruction of Jerusalem and the temple. . . . How could these important messages regarding the temple have been delivered in any other land? For His own mortal ministry He chose the land with the temple.

VOLUNTARY SERVICE

If any man serve me, let him follow me;
and where I am, there shall also my servant be:
if any man serve me, him will my Father honour.

JOHN 12:26

We need to remember constantly that the Lord leads His Church through volunteers. Jesus Christ voluntarily chose to follow the Father's plan and become the Savior and Redeemer of all mankind. When we serve as volunteers in His Church, we follow the example of Jesus Christ. All who are called to be leaders in His Church—male and female—are volunteers. We should express gratitude for our brothers and sisters who accept a call and serve voluntarily.

LIGHT AND TRUTH

And truth is knowledge of things as they are,
and as they were, and as they are to come.

DOCTRINE AND COVENANTS 93:24

An unchanging principle is that of truth. Scripture reminds us that "the truth abideth forever and ever" (Doctrine and Covenants 1:39). Even though one's understanding of the truth may be fragmentary, truth itself does not change.

Everlasting truth and wisdom come from the Lord. The first truth ever taught to man came directly from Deity. From generation to generation, God has given additional light. Whether truth comes from a laboratory of science or directly by revelation, truth is embraced by the gospel.

FAITH AND EDUCATION

A wise man will hear, and will increase learning; and a
man of understanding shall attain unto wise counsels.

PROVERBS 1:5

I do have a deep and abiding faith in Him and His son, Jesus Christ. Education has increased that faith. As I have spent forty years of my life in the study of one of God's greatest creations, the human body, I know that this marvelous instrument is of divine origin. The anatomy, the physiology, the protective mechanisms, the healing powers—all are so well constructed and function so beautifully. It is as evident to me that they are the products of a divine creator as it must be for an astronomer to reach the same conclusion as he studies the endless phenomenon of the stars in the heavens. Furthering education need not challenge, but should increase your faith.

COURAGE NOT TO GIVE UP

Be strong and of a good courage, fear not, nor be afraid of them: for the Lord thy God, he it is that doth go with thee; he will not fail thee, nor forsake thee.

DEUTERONOMY 31:6

You will have days when you will be thoroughly discouraged. So pray for courage not to give up! You will need that strength because it will become less and less popular to be a Latter-day Saint. Sadly, some who you thought were your friends will betray you. And some things will simply seem unfair.

However, I promise you that as you follow Jesus Christ, you will find sustained peace and true joy. As you keep your covenants with increasing precision, and as you defend the Church and kingdom of God on the earth today, the Lord will bless you with strength and wisdom to accomplish the impossible.

DIRECTION FROM GOD

*But he knoweth the way that I take: when he
hath tried me, I shall come forth as gold.*

JOB 23:10

I promise *you*—not the person sitting next to you, but
you—that, wherever you are in the world, wherever you
are on the covenant path—even if, at this moment, you
are not centered *on* the path—I promise you that if
you will sincerely and persistently do the spiritual work
needed to develop the crucial, spiritual skill of learning
how to hear the whisperings of the Holy Ghost, you will
have *all* the direction you will ever need in your life. You
will be given answers to your questions in the Lord's
own way and in His own time. And don't forget the
counsel of your parents and Church leaders. They are
also seeking revelation in your behalf.

When you know your life is being directed by God,
regardless of the challenges and disappointments that
may and will come, you will feel joy and peace.

NOVEMBER

How beautiful upon the mountains
are the feet of him that bringeth
good tidings, that publisheth peace;
that bringeth good tidings of good,
that publisheth salvation; that saith
unto Zion, Thy God reigneth!

ISAIAH 52:7

ABILITY TO FORGIVE

Be ye therefore merciful, as your Father also is merciful.
Judge not, and ye shall not be judged: condemn not, and ye
shall not be condemned: forgive, and ye shall be forgiven.

LUKE 6:36–37

Another gift the Savior offers you is the ability to *forgive*. Through His infinite Atonement, you can forgive those who have hurt you and who may never accept responsibility for their cruelty to you.

It is usually easy to forgive one who sincerely and humbly seeks your forgiveness. But the Savior will grant you the ability to forgive anyone who has mistreated you in any way. Then their hurtful acts can no longer canker your soul.

HIS ETERNAL PERSPECTIVE

Who shall separate us from the love of Christ? shall
tribulation, or distress, or persecution, or famine, or
nakedness, or peril, or sword? . . . Nay, in all these things
we are more than conquerors through him that loved us.

ROMANS 8:35, 37

In this global climate of economic instability, spiritual degradation, and unanticipated acts of terror, we need not fear. We can learn lessons from the very history that we research and teach. It is often at the time of uncertainty, oppression, or even tragedy that teachings of the Lord come, or become more evident. Think of the circumstances at Gethsemane, the Sacred Grove, and at Liberty Jail!

In his wretched experience in Liberty Jail, the Prophet Joseph Smith prayed fervently for relief. How did the Lord answer those prayers? By changing the Prophet's perspective! "All these things shall give thee experience, and shall be for thy good" (Doctrine and Covenants 122:7). So we, too, will be able to endure our trials by viewing them as the Lord would see them from His celestial and eternal perspective.

WHAT IS TRUE

For the Lord shall be thy confidence,
and shall keep thy foot from being taken.

PROVERBS 3:26

It is imperative that you know God's laws. They control *this* universe and multitudes of others. When divine laws are broken, consequences follow. Even though our hearts ache for those who break God's laws, penalties must be paid. Divine law must be obeyed. . . .

While the world is filled with uncertainty, there need not be uncertainty in *your* heart and mind about what is true and what is not. Uncertainty is born of imperfect or unknown information. As an Apostle, I plead with you to learn God's irrevocable laws. Learn them by study and by faith.

THE WILL OF THE LORD

*Teach me to do thy will; for thou art my God: thy spirit
is good; lead me into the land of uprightness.*

PSALM 143:10

Not all of our prayers will be answered as we might wish. Occasionally the answer will be no. We should not be surprised. Loving mortal parents do not say yes to every request of their children. . . . We should pray in accord with the will of our Heavenly Father. He wants to test us, to strengthen us, and to help us achieve our full potential. When the Prophet Joseph Smith was held in Liberty Jail, he pled for relief. His prayers were answered with an explanation: "All these things shall give thee experience, and shall be for thy good" (Doctrine and Covenants 122:7).

A FIRM FOUNDATION OF FAITH

He that loveth not knoweth not God; for God is love.

1 JOHN 4:8

Love the Lord with a firm foundation of faith. Let it be the base upon which you stand and from which you climb. That love will provide power for you to love your neighbors and to help them. It will assuage any baser emotion of envy and attenuate immature passions for greed or power, control or unrighteous dominion.

Enlightened with love of the Lord, no longer will you be inclined to command with "directive" leadership. Your style will change to one of concerned "participative" leadership when you apply the Golden Rule.

But without a conviction that the Lord lives and loves us, and will judge us, there would be politics without principle, industry without morality, science without humanity, and knowledge without wisdom.

FORGING CHARACTER

*God forbid that I should justify you: till I die I
will not remove mine integrity from me.*

JOB 27:5

As you work during the productive years of life,
whether at home or in the field, in the factory or at a
workbench, reputation is built and character is forged as
you develop self-mastery. Faithful payment of tithing is
part of that process. It defends you against dishonesty or
shabby temptations. Courageous accountability for your
own actions becomes a cherished prize.

THE GARDEN OF MARRIAGE

Let the husband render unto the wife due benevolence:
and likewise also the wife unto the husband.

1 CORINTHIANS 7:3

Taking time to talk is essential to keep lines of communication intact. If marriage is a prime relationship in life, it deserves prime time! Yet less important appointments are often given priority, leaving only leftover moments for listening to precious partners.

Keeping the garden of marriage well cultivated and free from weeds of neglect requires the time and commitment of love. It is not only a pleasant privilege, it is a scriptural requirement with promise of eternal glory.

ETERNAL PERFECTION

And he said unto them, Go ye, and tell that fox,
Behold, I cast out devils, and I do cures to day and to
morrow, and the third day I shall be perfected.

LUKE 13:32

Think of that! The sinless, errorless Lord—already perfect by our mortal standards—proclaimed His own state of perfection yet to be in the future. His *eternal* perfection would follow His Resurrection and receipt of "all power . . . in heaven and in earth" (Matthew 28:18).

The perfection that the Savior envisions for us is much more than errorless performance. It is the eternal expectation as expressed by the Lord in His great intercessory prayer to His Father—that we might be made perfect and be able to dwell with them in the eternities ahead.

The Lord's entire work and glory pertains to the immortality and eternal life of each human being. He came into the world to do the will of His Father, who sent Him. His sacred responsibility was foreseen before the Creation and was foretold by all His holy prophets since the world began.

A LIGHT TO HIS PEOPLE

Let no man despise thy youth; but be thou an
example of the believers, in word, in conversation,
in charity, in spirit, in faith, in purity.

1 TIMOTHY 4:12

How you deal with life's trials is part of the development of your faith. Strength comes when you remember that you have a divine nature, an inheritance of infinite worth. The Lord has reminded you, your children, and your grandchildren that you are lawful heirs, that you have been reserved in heaven for your specific time and place to be born, to grow and become His standard bearers and covenant people. As you walk in the Lord's path of righteousness, you will be blessed to continue in His goodness and be a light and a savior unto His people.

FOCUS FIXED
ON ETERNITY

He that overcometh shall inherit all things; and
I will be his God, and he shall be my son.

REVELATION 21:7

Recently I visited the home of a man terminally ill. The stake president introduced me to the man's family. His wife demonstrated such focus when she asked for a blessing for her dying husband—not for healing, but for peace, not for a miracle, but for ability to abide to the end. She could see from an eternal viewpoint, not merely from the perspective of one weighted with the responsibilities of her husband's day-to-day care.

Elsewhere, a mother with focus nurtures her son, crippled for the whole of this life. Daily she thanks her Heavenly Father for the privilege of laboring in love with a child for whom mortality's vale of tears will be mercifully brief. Her focus is fixed on eternity. With celestial sight, trials impossible to change become possible to endure.

FOR LEARNING
AND PROFIT

*And upon these I write the things of my soul, and many of the
scriptures which are engraven upon the plates of brass. For my
soul delighteth in the scriptures, and my heart pondereth them,
and writeth them for the learning and the profit of my children.*

2 NEPHI 4:15

Each individual who prayerfully studies the Book of
Mormon can also receive a testimony of its divinity. In
addition, this book can help with personal problems in a
very real way. Do you want to get rid of a bad habit? Do
you want to improve relationships in your family? Do you
want to increase your spiritual capacity? Read the Book
of Mormon! It will bring you closer to the Lord and His
loving power. He who fed a multitude with five loaves
and two fishes—He who helped the blind to see and the
lame to walk—can also bless you! He has promised that
those who live by the precepts of this book "shall receive
a crown of eternal life" (Doctrine and Covenants 20:14).

EXPRESS GRATITUDE

And he who receiveth all things with thankfulness shall be made glorious; and the things of this earth shall be added unto him, even an hundred fold, yea, more.

DOCTRINE AND COVENANTS 78:19

I thought of some people I know who are just as oblivious to their Creator and their true "bread of life" (John 6:35). They live from day to day without an awareness of God and His goodness unto them.

How much better it would be if all could be more aware of God's providence and love and express gratitude to Him. Ammon taught, "Let us give thanks to [God], for he doth work righteousness forever" (Alma 26:8). Our degree of gratitude is a measure of our love for Him.

God is the Father of our spirits. He has a glorified, perfected body of flesh and bone. We lived with Him in heaven before we were born. And when He created us physically, we were created in the image of God, each with a personal body.

THE FUTURE

For by my Spirit will I enlighten them, and by my power will I make known unto them the secrets of my will—yea, even those things which eye has not seen, nor ear heard, nor yet entered into the heart of man.

DOCTRINE AND COVENANTS 76:10

Today, the Lord's work in The Church of Jesus Christ of Latter-day Saints is moving forward at an accelerated pace. The Church will have an unprecedented, unparalleled future. . . .

Remember that the fulness of Jesus Christ's ministry lies in the future. The prophecies of His Second Coming have yet to be fulfilled. We are just building up to the climax of this last dispensation—when the Savior's Second Coming becomes a reality.

THINKING BEYOND

Yea, blessed is this people who are willing to bear my name;
for in my name shall they be called; and they are mine.

MOSIAH 26:18

We need to think beyond the tasks of each day or the next hurdle ahead. We need to do more than the deeds scheduled in our daily calendars or planners. Now is the time to take the name of the Lord upon us and become more like Him. We really can rise to the great potential within us. We can look for spiritual achievement as we prepare for days ahead.

SIGNIFICANT CONSEQUENCES

Wherefore, men are free according to the flesh; and all things are given them which are expedient unto man. And they are free to choose liberty and eternal life, through the great Mediator of all men, or to choose captivity and death, according to the captivity and power of the devil.

2 NEPHI 2:27

Even though peaceful conditions seem to prevail here, we are still at war. That war is not between nations. It is a war between the forces of God and the forces of the adversary. This conflict began before the world was created. It began with the war in heaven. On God's side was Jesus Christ, foreordained to be the Savior of the World. The opposing forces were and are led by Satan.

Our Heavenly Father's plan has allowed for that conflict to exist. Why? It is allowed so that we could exercise our precious gift of agency and make our own choices between good and evil.

This is the conflict in which we are all enlisted. As we choose good over evil, we are the Lord's advocates for joy. . . . In contrast, Satan wants us to be miserable, just as he is. The choice between joy and misery would seem to be obvious. Yet the consequences are of eternal significance.

PROPHETS OF GOD

Since the day that your fathers came forth out of the land of Egypt unto this day I have even sent unto you all my servants the prophets, daily rising up early and sending them.

JEREMIAH 7:25

A prophet is one called of God to speak for Him. Throughout history, prophets have testified of Jesus Christ and have taught His gospel. Revelation is communicated from God through prophets to his children. For the entire Church, revelation comes from God to His prophets and apostles. Sacred scriptures are priceless records of revelation to previous prophets. For each worthy member, revelation comes through the Holy Ghost for one's personal guidance and blessing.

CHOSEN AND ORDAINED

*Ye have not chosen me, but I have chosen you, and
ordained you, that ye should go and bring forth fruit, and
that your fruit should remain: that whatsoever ye shall
ask of the Father in my name, he may give it you.*

JOHN 15:16

The priesthood may be defined as the power and authority of God delegated to man, to minister for the salvation of men. The priesthood is without beginning and without end. Adam possessed its presidential power prior to the creation of the earth and later conferred it on others. Those called to bear the priesthood have been foreordained to that calling (see Alma 13:3–9).

STRENGTH
AND GUIDANCE

Let us therefore come boldly unto the throne of grace, that we may obtain mercy, and find grace to help in time of need.

HEBREWS 4:16

Know that, like the stripling warriors, you can be preserved in your hardships. You can overcome past temptations and unworthy behavior if you put your trust in God and the teachings you receive from parents [and leaders].

Please understand that protection and strength are available to you. Prayer, the influence of the Holy Ghost, scriptures, priesthood blessings, appropriate fasting, and companions can all provide strength and guidance for you during your times of need. . . .

The Savior is not disappointed with anyone who earnestly seeks to repent. He is grateful, as are we, for the faith they have exercised . . . to repent and seek forgiveness through the Atonement of Jesus Christ.

PRAYERFUL GREETINGS

Thou, even thou, art Lord alone; thou hast made heaven, the heaven of heavens, with all their host, the earth, and all things that are therein, the seas, and all that is therein, and thou preservest them all; and the host of heaven worshippeth thee.

NEHEMIAH 9:6

Spiritual self-esteem begins with the realization that each new morning is a gift from God. Even the air we breathe is a loving loan from Him. He preserves us from day to day and supports us from one moment to another.

Therefore, our first noble deed of the morning should be a humble prayer of gratitude. . . . I did not fully appreciate the significance of prayerful greetings until I became a father myself. I am so grateful that our children never gave their mother or dad the silent treatment. Now I sense how our Heavenly Father may appreciate our prayers, morning and night. But I can imagine the pangs of his sorrow because of silence from any of his children. To me, such ingratitude seems comparable to sullen goldfish oblivious to kind providers who sprinkle food in their bowl.

ANSWERS TO PRAYERS

Call unto me, and I will answer thee, and shew thee
great and mighty things, which thou knowest not.
JEREMIAH 33:3

Our loving Father in Heaven hears our prayers. Sometimes we need to take a little while after we have prayed to listen to the answers, because the answers are not audible to our hearing. The answers come in the way of thoughts, ideas, and instruction, in some cases.

. . . I have always been a praying person, but the answers to my prayers are now coming in the middle of the night—usually when I'm fast asleep. When I was a medical doctor, I used to get a lot of phone calls at night. Now my phone doesn't ring at night, but I still get calls: instructions from the Lord for me and for His children. That modality of prayer is very important.

MORTAL PERFECTION

For I, the Lord, will judge all men according to their works, according to the desire of their hearts.

DOCTRINE AND COVENANTS 137:9

Scriptures have described Noah, Seth, and Job as *perfect* men (see Genesis 6:9; Doctrine and Covenants 107:43; Job 1:1). No doubt the same term might apply to a large number of faithful disciples in various dispensations. . . .

This does not mean that these people never made mistakes or never had need of correction. The process of perfection includes challenges to overcome and steps to repentance that may be very painful. There is a proper place for chastisement in the molding of character, for we know that "whom the Lord loveth he chasteneth" (Hebrews 12:6).

Mortal perfection can be achieved as we try to perform every duty, keep every law, and strive to be as perfect in our sphere as our Heavenly Father is in His. If we do the best we can, the Lord will bless us according to our deeds and the desires of our hearts.

EMULATING THE LORD

Now the end of the commandment is charity out of a pure heart, and of a good conscience, and of faith unfeigned.

1 TIMOTHY 1:5

Relationships with neighbors, friends, and associates will be enhanced as we approach them with "the pure love of Christ" (Moroni 7:47). A desire to emulate the Lord provides powerful motivation for good. Our craving for compassion will cause us to act in accord with the Golden Rule. By so doing, we will find joy in feeding the poor, clothing the naked, or doing volunteer work of worth.

Service to neighbors takes on new stature when we first look to God. In the Church, when priesthood and auxiliary leaders face their congregations, quorums, and classes as would the Lord, they learn that it does not matter *where* they serve, but *how*. Position in the Church does not exalt anyone, but faithfulness does.

A WORK TO DO

And this they did, vouching and covenanting with God,
that . . . rather than take away from a brother they would
give unto him; and rather than spend their days in idleness
they would labor abundantly with their hands.

ALMA 24:18

Whether married or single, you will all have work to do. I hope it will be enjoyable. It's nice to bounce out of bed each morning eager to enjoy a day's work, and it is especially gratifying when we can bless the lives of others. But please remember: You work to sustain life; you don't live to sustain work.

MESSAGES FROM HEAVENLY FATHER

I glory in plainness; I glory in truth; I glory in my Jesus, for he hath redeemed my soul from hell.

2 NEPHI 33:6

Repeatedly, past prophets have declared "great and marvelous things unto the people, which they did not believe" (Ether 12:5). It's no different in our day. Through the years, great and marvelous things have been heard from dedicated pulpits across the earth. Yet most people do *not* embrace these truths—either because they do not know where to look for them or because they are listening to those who do not have the whole truth or because they have rejected truth in favor of worldly pursuits.

The adversary is clever. For millennia he has been making good look evil and evil look good. His messages tend to be loud, bold, and boastful. However, messages from our Heavenly Father are strikingly different. He communicates simply, quietly, and with such stunning plainness that we cannot misunderstand Him.

THE CRUCIBLE OF ADVERSITY

Therefore I take pleasure in infirmities, in reproaches, in necessities, in persecutions, in distresses for Christ's sake: for when I am weak, then am I strong.

2 CORINTHIANS 12:10

The pioneers understood hardship. They understood trial. . . . One thing all these people had in common, in their search for freedom to worship, was the knowledge that God often tutors His people through travail. A schooling in hardship, persecution, and sacrifice would refine weakness from their souls, leaving them only the pure mettle of loftiest character, and sterling faith, fully tested. They knew that God does not work out His purposes through pampered victims of affluence or riotous living. History had taught them that, in His work, He used great crises, employing affliction and privation to forge spiritual spines of steel. Indeed, they knew that God shapes His servants in the crucible of adversity, never fashioning them in the hothouse of ease and luxury.

ASK THE MISSIONARIES

Do ye not remember the things which the Lord hath said?—If ye will not harden your hearts, and ask me in faith, believing that ye shall receive, with diligence in keeping my commandments, surely these things shall be made known unto you.

1 NEPHI 15:11

Some of you are members but not presently participating. You love the Lord and often think of returning to His fold. But you don't know how to start. I suggest that you ask the missionaries! They can help you! . . .

Some of you may feel that life is busy and frenetic, yet down deep in your heart you feel a gnawing emptiness, without direction or purpose. Ask the missionaries! They can help you! They can help you to learn more about the true purpose of life—why you are here on earth and where you are going after death. You can learn how the restored gospel of Jesus Christ will bless your life beyond anything you can presently even imagine.

SAVIORS ON MOUNT ZION

And he shall go before him in the spirit and power of
Elias, to turn the hearts of the fathers to the children,
and the disobedient to the wisdom of the just; to
make ready a people prepared for the Lord.

LUKE 1:17

Family history research, ancestral pictures, and histories are very interesting and important. But, please remember, they are a means to an end. They are not an end in itself. The end is the endowment and the sealing ordinances of the temple. We could compile volumes about our ancestors, but without their ordinances being completed, we will not have served them as they hope and pray we will. We are to be their saviors on Mount Zion.

CHILDREN OF GOD

Therefore all things whatsoever ye would that men should do to you, do ye even so to them: for this is the law and the prophets.

MATTHEW 7:12

Together we live on this earth, which is to be tended, subdued, and shared with gratitude. Each of us can help to make life in this world a more pleasant experience. . . . Together we may stand, intolerant of transgression but tolerant of neighbors with differences they hold sacred. Our beloved brothers and sisters throughout the world are *all* children of God. He is our Father.

EMPLOYING THE UNLIKELY

*For verily I say unto you, blessed is he that keepeth
my commandments, whether in life or in death;
and he that is faithful in tribulation, the reward of
the same is greater in the kingdom of heaven.*

DOCTRINE AND COVENANTS 58:2

As a medical doctor, I have known the face of adversity. I have seen much of death and dying, suffering and sorrow. I also remember the plight of students overwhelmed by their studies and of those striving to learn a foreign language. And I recall the fatigue and frustration felt by young parents with children in need. Amidst circumstances seemingly impossible, I have also experienced the joyous relief that comes when one's understanding is deepened by scriptural insight.

The Lord has often chosen to instruct His people in their times of trial. Scriptures show that some of His lasting lessons have been taught with examples terrible as war, commonplace as childbearing, or obvious as hazards of deep water. His teachings are frequently based on common understandings, but with uncommon results.

CORRODING CANKER
OF THE SPIRIT

*For verily, verily I say unto you, he that hath the spirit
of contention is not of me, but is of the devil, who is
the father of contention, and he stirreth up the hearts
of men to contend with anger, one with another.*

3 NEPHI 11:29

The Savior's peace is not necessarily political; His peace
is personal. But that spirit of inner peace is driven away
by contention. Contention does not usually begin as
strife between countries. More often, it starts with an
individual, for we can contend within ourselves over
simple matters of right and wrong. From there, contention can infect neighbors and nations like a spreading
sore.

As we dread any disease that undermines the health
of the body, so should we deplore contention, which is a
corroding canker of the spirit.

DECEMBER

And he cometh into the world that
he may save all men if they will
hearken unto his voice; for behold,
he suffereth the pains of all men, yea,
the pains of every living creature,
both men, women, and children,
who belong to the family of Adam.

2 NEPHI 9:21

TRUTH DRAWS US TO JESUS CHRIST

Draw near unto me and I will draw near unto you;
seek me diligently and ye shall find me; ask, and ye shall
receive; knock, and it shall be opened unto you.

DOCTRINE AND COVENANTS 88:63

There is divine light and power in truth. The plain and simple words of truth stir our souls. If we truly hear them, if we walk in the ways of truth according to the laws of God, the words of truth draw us to the Lord Jesus Christ. . . . If we continue to walk in truth, the Holy Ghost—"the Spirit of truth" (John 15:26)—will be our companion. The truth will be in us, in our hearts and minds, in our character and being, and it will abound in us, growing "brighter and brighter until the perfect day" (Doctrine and Covenants 50:24).

SACRED GIFTS OF WOMEN

Behold thou hast a gift, and blessed art thou because of thy gift. Remember it is sacred and cometh from above.

DOCTRINE AND COVENANTS 6:10

My dear sisters, whatever your calling, whatever your circumstances, we need your impressions, your insights, and your inspiration. We need you to speak up and speak out in ward and stake councils. . . . Married or single, you sisters possess distinctive capabilities and special intuition you have received as gifts from God. . . .

Attacks against the Church, its doctrine, and our way of life are going to increase. Because of this, we need women who have a bedrock understanding of the doctrine of Christ and who will use that understanding to teach and help raise a sin-resistant generation. We need women who can detect deception in all of its forms. We need women who know how to access the power that God makes available to covenant keepers and who express their beliefs with confidence and charity.

THE GATHERING
OF ISRAEL

And even so will I gather mine elect from the
four quarters of the earth, even as many as will
believe in me, and hearken unto my voice.

DOCTRINE AND COVENANTS 33:6

The gathering of Israel is the most important thing taking place on earth today. Nothing else compares in magnitude, nothing else compares in importance, nothing else compares in majesty. And if you choose to, if you want to, you can be a big part of it. You can be a big part of something big, something grand, something majestic!

When we speak of the *gathering,* we are simply saying this fundamental truth: every one of our Heavenly Father's children, on both sides of the veil, deserves to hear the message of the restored gospel of Jesus Christ. They decide for themselves if they want to know more.

FAITH FORTIFIED
THROUGH PRAYER

*Wherefore, my beloved brethren, pray unto the Father
with all the energy of heart, that ye may be filled
with this love, which he hath bestowed upon all
who are true followers of his Son, Jesus Christ.*

MORONI 7:48

Many may profess a measure of faith in God, but without sincere repentance, faith cannot be fully operative. . . . Faith, repentance, and obedience will qualify you for sublime gifts of justice and mercy, which are bestowed upon those worthy of the blessings of the Atonement.

Yes, every test, every trial, every challenge and hardship you endure is an opportunity to further develop your faith.

Faith can be fortified through prayer. Prayer is the powerful key to making decisions, not only concerning your physical body, but concerning all other important aspects of your life. Humbly seek the Lord in prayer with a sincere heart and real intent, and He will help you.

STRENGTH TO SUBMIT

Humble yourselves in the sight of the
Lord, and he shall lift you up.

JAMES 4:10

Not an age in life passes without temptation, trial, or torment experienced through your physical body. But as you prayerfully develop self-mastery, desires of the flesh may be subdued. And when that has been achieved, you may have the strength to submit to your Heavenly Father, as did Jesus, who said, "Not my will, but thine, be done" (Luke 22:42).

THE PERSON YOU CAN BECOME

But we all, with open face beholding as in a glass the glory of the Lord, are changed into the same image from glory to glory, even as by the Spirit of the Lord.

2 CORINTHIANS 3:18

I have learned that a doctor's ultimate destination is not in the hospital. For a lawyer, it is not in the courtroom. For a pilot, it is not in the cockpit of a large jet. A person's chosen occupation is only a *means* to an end; it is not an end in itself. One's true identity should not be defined by one's occupation.

Your true identity is established by *becoming* the person you can become—the person God wants you to be. The day will come when your working days will end. The work that will have supported you and your family one day will be behind you. On your final graduation day, when you finally leave this frail existence, what you will have become will matter much more than merely your career. From an eternal perspective, who you really are is far more important than is what you did.

STAND OUT

And the Lord hath avouched thee this day to be his
peculiar people, as he hath promised thee, and that
thou shouldest keep all his commandments.

DEUTERONOMY 26:18

Stand out; be different from the world. You and I know that you are to be a light to the world. Therefore, the Lord needs you to look like, sound like, act like, and dress like a true disciple of Jesus Christ. Yes, you are living in the world, but you have very different standards from the world to help you avoid the stain of the world.

With the Holy Ghost as your companion, you can see right through the celebrity culture that has smitten our society. You can be smarter than previous generations have ever been. And if you are sometimes called "weird," wear that distinction as a badge of honor and be happy that your light is shining brightly in this ever-darkening world!

Set a standard for the rest of the world! Embrace being different!

STAYING WITH THE LORD

And now behold, I say unto you, my brethren, if ye have
experienced a change of heart, and if ye have felt to sing the
song of redeeming love, I would ask, can ye feel so now?

ALMA 5:26

Faith, repentance, baptism, a testimony, and enduring conversion lead to the healing power of the Lord.
Baptism is a covenant act—a sign of a commitment and
a promise. Testimony develops when the Holy Ghost
gives conviction to the earnest seeker of the truth. True
testimony fosters faith; it promotes repentance and obedience to God's commandments. Testimony engenders
enthusiasm to serve God and fellow human beings.
Conversion means "to turn with." Conversion is a turn-
ing *from* the ways of the world *to*, and staying *with*, the
ways of the Lord. Conversion includes repentance and
obedience. Conversion brings a mighty change of heart.

MANNER OF
JESUS CHRIST'S BAPTISM

And now, if the Lamb of God, he being holy, should
have need to be baptized by water, to fulfil all
righteousness, O then, how much more need have we,
being unholy, to be baptized, yea, even by water!

2 NEPHI 31:5

Much of the Holy Land is desert with very little water. Because water was scarce and precious, it became the object of special lessons taught by the Lord.

The River Jordan was the site Jesus chose for His baptism by John to "fulfil all righteousness" (Matthew 3:15). Is it significant that this sacred ordinance was performed in virtually the lowest body of fresh water on the planet? Could He have selected a better place to symbolize the humble depths to which He went and from which He rose? By example, he taught us that He literally descended beneath all things to rise above all things. Surely, being baptized after the manner of his baptism signifies that through our obedience and effort we, too, can come from the depths to ascend to lofty heights of our own destiny.

CONNECT WITH THE LORD

For behold, in my name are they called; and if they know me they shall come forth, and shall have a place eternally at my right hand.

MOSIAH 26:24

A missionary's highest need is to connect with the Lord. He is your Creator. This is His work and you are His servants. He loves you and wants you to be successful. You have been called to teach His gospel. You have been commissioned to bring souls unto Him. As His messengers, you will teach best when you are connected to Him and moved upon by His Spirit—connected with the power of the Holy Ghost. . . .

To connect with the Lord, make room in your heart and mind for Him. Learn from the scripture that says, "For how knoweth a man the master whom he has not served, and who is a stranger unto him, and is far from the thoughts and intents of his heart?" (Mosiah 5:13). Don't ever allow the Lord to be a stranger to you.

TRUTH AND MORE

Let not mercy and truth forsake thee: bind them about
thy neck; write them upon the table of thine heart.

PROVERBS 3:3

Imagine a surgeon who has just operated upon a patient and found cancer . . . beyond cure. With this knowledge, the surgeon approaches the family and the patient and coldly announces that the patient has advanced cancer, that he is beyond hope and is doomed to die. While discharging his duty to share that information, the surgeon has told the truth, but with utter abandon has then walked away from the turmoil that "truth" has left in its wake.

Another surgeon, with that same information and with compassion, approaches the family, speaks the truth, and then mercifully indicates that, even though the road ahead will be difficult and challenging, the patient and the family will not be forsaken. They will be supported with all the resources available to him as their caring physician.

Important as truth is, often we need truth *and more*.

LEADERSHIP BY EXAMPLE

The integrity of the upright shall guide them.
PROVERBS 11:3

Leadership by example is paramount. . . . Integrity, honesty, and compassion bring credibility to character. People enjoy making commitments to leaders in whom they have confidence. An effective leader practices conservation of time. His eyes search for new developments. He builds on the strength of his colleagues and builds them in the process. He deals with his problems without dwelling upon them. He feeds upon opportunities and inspires others with positive expressions of his vision for the future.

PART OF HIS FOLD

*He numbereth his sheep, and they know him; and
there shall be one fold and one shepherd; and he shall
feed his sheep, and in him they shall find pasture.*

1 NEPHI 22:25

To anyone so struggling, know that you can be redeemed. You can be made whole. . . . Follow the Good Shepherd, brothers and sisters, and be a positive part of His fold. Remember that His Church is not intended to be a sanctuary for the sinless; it is to be a hospital of hope for those who want to get well. Do whatever you have to do to be fully in the fold. For some that means to live with greater faith, to believe more. For others it means to repent. For all of us it means to live more by the promptings of the Holy Ghost and to "press forward with a steadfastness in Christ, having a perfect brightness of hope, and a love of God and of all men" (2 Nephi 31:20).

A TRUE MILLENNIAL

*Prepare ye, prepare ye for that which is
to come, for the Lord is nigh.*

DOCTRINE AND COVENANTS 1:12

A true millennial is one who taught and who was taught the gospel of Jesus Christ premortally and who made covenants there with our Heavenly Father about courageous things—even *morally* courageous things—that he or she would do while here on earth.

A true millennial is a man or woman whom God trusted enough to send to earth during the most compelling dispensation in the history of this world. A true millennial is a man or woman who lives now to help prepare the people of this world for the Second Coming of Jesus Christ and His millennial reign. Make no mistake about it—you were born to be a true millennial.

THE LORD JESUS CHRIST

And my spirit hath rejoiced in God my Saviour.
LUKE 1:47

I express special gratitude to the Lord Jesus Christ. I am thankful for His loving-kindness and for His open invitation to come unto Him. I marvel at His matchless power to heal. I testify of Jesus Christ as the Master Healer. It is but one of many attributes that characterize His incomparable life.

Jesus is the Christ, the Messiah, the Son of God, the Creator, the great Jehovah, the promised Immanuel, our atoning Savior and Redeemer, our Advocate with the Father, our great Exemplar. And one day we will stand before Him as our just and merciful Judge.

EXAMPLES OF THE SAVIOR

And when he had called the people unto him with his disciples
also, he said unto them, Whosoever will come after me,
let him deny himself, and take up his cross, and follow me.

MARK 8:34

You and I are to bear witness; we are to minister; we are to enlighten; we are to be an example to all who come within our sphere of influence. This privilege is ours, twenty-four hours a day, 365 days a year—even on vacation. . . . Your most sincere sign of adoration of Jesus is your emulation of Him. You know of Him. You know of His divine parentage. You know of His mission and ministry in mortality. You know of Him, not by direct visitation, but through the testimony of the Holy Ghost.

TIME OF TEARS

They that sow in tears shall reap in joy.

PSALM 126:5

Christmas is a time for families, a time of joy, a time of love and cheer. For many of us, it is also a time of tears. Tender recollections come of loved ones who were a vital part of Christmases past. The older I get, the greater are the memories of those who now live on the other side of the veil. I never apologize for those tears. A good cry at Christmastime is a sacred symbol of love.

HIS PEOPLE

O death, where is thy sting?
O grave, where is thy victory?

1 CORINTHIANS 15:55

When we realize that we are children of the covenant, we know who we are and what God expects of us. His law is written in our hearts. He is our God and we are His people. Committed children of the covenant remain steadfast, even in the midst of adversity. When that doctrine is deeply implanted in our hearts, even the sting of death is soothed and out spiritual stamina is strengthened.

BREAD OF LIFE

*Come unto me and ye shall partake of the fruit
of the tree of life; yea, ye shall eat and drink of
the bread and the waters of life freely.*

ALMA 5:34

After millennia of preparation, the long awaited event occurred. Jesus Christ was born among men. No wonder angelic choirs sang as they knew that extended centuries of death and darkness were to be relieved by the Atonement, which was finally to come through this Babe of Bethlehem.

Why Bethlehem? Is there symbolic significance in the meaning of the name *Bethlehem,* which in Hebrew means "house of bread"? The Great Provider declared Himself to be the "bread of life" (John 6:48). How appropriate it was that He, the "bread of life," was to come from the "house of bread."

JESUS CHRIST BRINGS PEACE

The Lord is my light and my salvation; whom shall I fear?
the Lord is the strength of my life; of whom shall I be afraid?

PSALM 27:1

Jesus came to the earth to do what we could not do for ourselves. He brought hope, peace, light, and understanding to a dark and ignorant world. The miracle of His Resurrection gives real meaning to His birth. The great message of Christmas is not in the birth of Jesus Christ but in His death for us. The message of Christmas would be nothing without the message of Easter. But our knowledge of the Savior and Redeemer is meaningless unless we obey Him, keep His commandments, and qualify for all the blessings that He has in store for the faithful.

PRICELESS GIFTS

Thanks be unto God for his unspeakable gift.
2 CORINTHIANS 9:15

Just as there was no room for the Christ child at the inn at the time of His birth, with so many people, there is no place for Him in their hearts. The world He came to save has been so filled with trivia that little room has been left for the Lord and His righteousness. Many people have made room for sports and recreation, trinkets and toys, but the Prince of Peace—the Savior of mankind—is often forgotten.

At Christmastime we exchange gifts, but what have we done to show our appreciation to Him who created the entire earth with all of its beauty and abundance? How could we ignore Him who gave us life and all that sustains life? These priceless gifts come from Him. Wouldn't it be nice if we could improve our ways—as a gift to Him at Christmastime? If His stocking has been empty in our minds, what could we now give?

TRUE TESTIMONY

Behold, I am Jesus Christ the Son of God. I created the heavens
and the earth, and all things that in them are. I was with
the Father from the beginning. I am in the Father, and the
Father in me; and in me hath the Father glorified his name.

3 NEPHI 9:15

Each of us with a testimony of the Lord has the privilege in faith to know of His divine parentage and to testify that Jesus is the Son of the living God.

True testimony includes the fact that the Father and the Son appeared to the Prophet Joseph Smith, whose birth we commemorate on December 23. That testimony includes the fact that The Church of Jesus Christ of Latter-day Saints is true, led by the living Lord via prophecy and revelation through authorized administrators who receive and respond to direction from Him.

THE EVERLASTING GOSPEL

And after having received the record of the Nephites, yea, even my servant Joseph Smith, Jun., might have power to translate through the mercy of God, by the power of God, the Book of Mormon.

DOCTRINE AND COVENANTS 1:29

Through the Prophet Joseph Smith we have received . . . the Book of Mormon, which is another testament of Jesus Christ. It contains the fullness of the gospel of Jesus Christ, meaning it contains more information about the life, the mission, and the ministry of Jesus Christ than does any other book. From revelations given through the Prophet Joseph Smith, we know that the gospel did not originate in the meridian of time. It is everlasting. It was taught by Adam. . . . And it will be taught in that same purity by future prophets who will stand at the head of this Church.

THE FOCUS OF OUR LIVES

*Lift up your head and be of good cheer; for behold, the
time is at hand, and on this night shall the sign be given,
and on the morrow come I into the world, to show unto
the world that I will fulfil all that which I have caused
to be spoken by the mouth of my holy prophets.*

3 NEPHI 1:13

Life is filled with detours and dead ends, trials and
challenges of every kind. Each of us has likely had times
when distress, anguish, and despair almost consumed us.
Yet we are here to have joy?

Yes! The answer is a resounding yes! . . . Saints can
be happy under every circumstance. We can feel joy
even while having a bad day, a bad week, or even a bad
year! . . .

The joy we feel has little to do with the circumstances
of our lives and everything to do with the focus of our
lives.

TRUE SPIRIT OF CHRISTMAS

And she shall bring forth a son, and thou shalt call his name Jesus: for he shall save his people from their sins.

MATTHEW 1:21

For many of us, December is a favorite month. It brings the joy of Christmas. Unfortunately, it is becoming a time of increasing commercial importance. It's also a time of overeating, overspending, and overdoing. . . . Any obsession with material things—Santa Claus or extravagant gifts—can smother out the sweet sights, sounds, and significance of Christmas. . . .

The true spirit of Christmas comes because of the Christ. Christmas bears His holy name, yet Jesus as the Christ is unknown by most people on this planet, where Christianity is a minority religion. That makes our responsibilities as emissaries of the Lord even more significant. We know who He is, and as His disciples, we know who we are and what we are to do. We are to bear His message to the world.

HIS GIFT OF LOVE

Love worketh no ill to his neighbour:
therefore love is the fulfilling of the law.

ROMANS 13:10

Jesus Christ gave you and me an unlimited capacity *to love*. That includes the capacity to love the unlovable and those who not only do *not* love you but presently persecute and despitefully use you (see Matthew 5:44–45).

With the Savior's help, we can learn to love as He loved. It may require a change of heart—most certainly a softening of our hearts—as we are tutored by the Savior how to really take care of each other. My dear brothers and sisters, we can truly minister in the Lord's way as we accept His gift of love.

Ask for the Lord's help to love those He needs you to love, including those for whom it is not always easy to feel affection. You may even want to ask God for His angels to walk with you where you presently do not want to tread.

CHRISTLIKE ATTRIBUTES

Therefore I would that ye should be perfect even as I,
or your Father who is in heaven is perfect.

3 NEPHI 12:48

Focus on becoming the person the Lord needs you to be. Strive to develop the spiritual attributes of faith, virtue, knowledge, temperance, patience, brotherly kindness, godliness, charity, humility, and diligence. These attributes are difficult to measure, but they constitute the substance of what the Lord hopes for each of you. Remember His counsel posed to us as a question: "What manner of men [and women] ought ye to be? Verily I say unto you, even as I am" (3 Nephi 27:27).

SCIENCE AND RELIGION

*The glory of God is intelligence, or,
in other words, light and truth.*

DOCTRINE AND COVENANTS 93:36

There is no conflict between science and religion. Conflict only arises from an incomplete knowledge of either science or religion, or both. . . . All truth is part of the gospel of Jesus Christ. Whether truth comes from a scientific laboratory or by revelation from the Lord, it is compatible. . . .

Research and education are religious responsibilities for members of The Church of Jesus Christ of Latter-day Saints, for we know that "the glory of God is intelligence" (Doctrine and Covenants 93:36). And our perspective is enlarged by knowing that "whatever principle of intelligence we attain unto in this life, it will rise with us in the resurrection" (Doctrine and Covenants 130:18).

OUR DEEPEST DESIRES

*Delight thyself also in the Lord; and he shall
give thee the desires of thine heart.*

PSALM 37:4

Our desires influence each of us in profound ways, not just here and now but beyond. Consider the significance of this statement from Alma: "[The Lord] granteth unto men *according to their desire*" (Alma 29:4; emphasis added).

Desire is important in this season of gift giving, when we are particularly mindful of the desires of those whom we love. During this season, I invite you to consider your own desires. What are your deepest desires? What do you really want to experience and accomplish in this life? Do you really want to become more and more like Jesus Christ? Do you really want to live with Heavenly Father and with your family forever and live as He lives?

FILLING OUR SPIRITUAL STOREHOUSES

Wherefore, treasure up wisdom in your bosoms, lest the wickedness of men reveal these things unto you by their wickedness, in a manner which shall speak in your ears with a voice louder than that which shall shake the earth; but if ye are prepared ye shall not fear.

DOCTRINE AND COVENANTS 38:30

Future trials could result from an accident, a natural disaster, or an unexpected personal heartache.

How can we endure such trials? . . . Of course, we can store our own reserves of food, water, and savings. But equally crucial is our need to fill our personal *spiritual* storehouses with faith, truth, and testimony.

Our ultimate quest in life is to prepare to meet our Maker. We do this by striving daily to become more like our Savior, Jesus Christ. And we do *that* as we repent daily and receive His cleaning, healing, and strengthening power. Then we can feel enduring peace and joy, even during turbulent times. This is exactly why the Lord has implored us to stand in holy places and "be not moved" (Doctrine and Covenants 87:8).

ENDURE TO THE END

Behold, I am the law, and the light. Look unto me,
and endure to the end, and ye shall live; for unto him
that endureth to the end will I give eternal life.

3 NEPHI 15:9

Energy is always required to provide lift over opposing forces. These same laws apply in our personal lives. Whenever an undertaking is begun, both the energy and the will to endure are essential. The winner of a five-kilometer race is declared at the end of *five* kilometers, not at one or two. If you board a bus to Boston, you don't get off at Burlington. If you want to gain an education, you don't drop out along the way—just as you don't pay to dine at an elegant restaurant only to walk away after sampling the salad.

Whatever your work may be, endure at the beginning, endure through opposing forces along the way, and endure to the end. Any job must be completed before you can enjoy the result for which you are working.

IMAGE CREDITS